STUDENT UNIT GUIDE

NEW EDITION

AQA A2 Law Unit 4

(Section C) Concepts of Law

Jennifer Currer and Peter Darwent
Series editor: Ian Yule

PHILIP ALLAN

Philip Allan, an imprint of Hodder Education, an Hachette UK company, Market Place, Deddington, Oxfordshire OX15 0SE

Orders
Bookpoint Ltd, 130 Milton Park, Abingdon, Oxfordshire OX14 4SB
tel: 01235 827827
fax: 01235 400401
e-mail: education@bookpoint.co.uk
Lines are open 9.00 a.m.–5.00 p.m., Monday to Saturday, with a 24-hour message answering service.
You can also order through the Philip Allan website: www.philipallan.co.uk

© Jennifer Currer and Peter Darwent 2013

ISBN 978-1-4441-7176-1

First printed 2013
Impression number 5 4 3 2
Year 2016 2015 2014 2013

Cover photo: blas/Fotolia

Typeset by Integra Software Services Pvt. Ltd., Pondicherry, India

Printed in Dubai

Hachette UK's policy is to use papers that are natural, renewable and recyclable products and made from wood grown in sustainable forests. The logging and manufacturing processes are expected to conform to the environmental regulations of the country of origin.

Contents

Getting the most from this book

Questions & Answers

Exam-style questions

Examiner comments on the questions

Tips on what you need to do to gain full marks, indicated by the icon ⊜.

Sample student answers

Practise the questions, then look at the student answers that follow each set of questions.

Examiner commentary on sample student answers

Find out how many marks each answer would be awarded in the exam and then read the examiner comments (preceded by the icon ⊜) following each student answer.

> Questions & Answers
>
> Question 1 **Law and morality**
>
> Discuss the relationship between law and morals and consider whether the debate on the relationship is still relevant. (30 marks)
>
> ⊜ This question requires you to 'discuss'. This means that you must present arguments and make comments about the relationship. In considering whether the debate is still relevant your task is to explain the nature of the Hart–Devlin debate and the views that were held and then to discuss whether there is evidence that the views presented in that debate are still relevant.
>
> **A-grade answer**
>
> Law is best described as rules made by authority. John Austin defined law as a command from a sovereign power. Law needs to be obeyed and is enforced through various sanctions. Morality is really values and principles rather than rules. Phil Harris defines a society's code of morality as a set of 'beliefs, values, principles and standards of behaviour'. Compliance is voluntary, though society can enforce moral codes informally, for example through disapproval and social rejection.
>
> There are a number of clear distinctions between law and morality. For example, law can always be proved by referring to the written record of it, whereas morality is opinion and open to dispute. Second, law can change instantly, for example homosexuality was legalised when the Sexual Offences Act 1967 came into effect and the ban on smoking in public places came into force on 1 July 2007. Morality on the other hand changes gradually. Finally, the sanctions for breaking the law are severe and could involve financial penalties or loss of liberty, while sanctions for breaking moral rules are usually social.
>
> But law and morality can also overlap. Sir John Salmond illustrated this by referring to overlapping circles. For example, there are many long-established legal rules that have a moral connection. These include the laws of murder and theft, which can be traced back to the Ten Commandments. For example, the Christian Bible and Jewish Torah state 'You shall not steal' and clearly the Theft Acts reflect this moral assertion. Also, changing moral views can lead to changes in the law. The legalisation of homosexuality and the banning of corporal punishment in schools are good examples of issues where general public attitudes had gradually changed and then the law changed, in part as a response to changed moral views. But the law can also be changed by judges. The case of R v R is a good example of the courts recognising that public morality had changed and deciding as a result that the previous legal position that a man could not be charged with raping his wife was no longer acceptable.
>
> ⊜ The answer begins with brief definitions and then explores the distinctions and the overlap between law and morality, using a range of examples. The answer goes on to discuss the difficulties the law has with following morality, which is an important aspect of the relationship.
>
> 64   AQA A2 Law

About this book

The AQA specification for the AS and A2 Law examinations is divided into four units. The guide for Unit 4 (Section C) Concepts of Law is different from the guides for Units 1, 2, 3 and Unit 4 (Sections A and B) Criminal Law (Offences Against Property) and Law of Tort. While it does contain specific material on the concepts of law and morality, law and justice, fault, judicial creativity and balancing conflicting interests, it is essential that, in order to demonstrate knowledge and understanding of these particular topics, you utilise appropriate knowledge of legal processes, institutions and substantive law gained in the study of the other units.

Within this unit, you are also required to criticise and evaluate existing legal rules and to consider them in wider contexts — social, ethical and political.

There are two sections to this guide:

- **Content Guidance** — this sets out the specification content for Unit 4 (Section C) Concepts of Law. It also contains references to different materials drawn from previously studied units to enable you to demonstrate a fuller understanding of each Unit 4 topic.
- **Questions and Answers** — this section provides sample A-grade answers to typical examination questions on each topic area. Examiner comments show how marks are awarded.

The Content Guidance section covers all the elements of the Unit 4 (Section C) Concepts of Law specification. Given the nature of this unit, it must be stressed that this section is not intended to be a comprehensive and detailed set of notes — the material needs to be supplemented by further reading from textbooks, and illustrative material needs to be augmented by considering relevant examples from materials previously studied. You are also strongly encouraged to read quality newspapers on a regular basis, and to use relevant legal websites and law journals, especially *A-level Law Review, New Law Journal* and other student magazines that give updates on legal developments.

Content Guidance

Law and morality

Characteristics of legal rules

Sir John Salmond, writing in the early twentieth century, described law as 'the body of principles recognised and applied by the state in the administration of justice'. John Austin, in his book *The Province of Jurisprudence*, defined it as a command issued from a sovereign power to an inferior and enforced by coercion. In Britain this sovereign power is Parliament, although legal rules are also made by judges.

Compliance with legal rules is compulsory. They are imposed on all members of society and must be obeyed. In Britain, everyone is bound by the **Offences Against the Person Act 1861**, s.20, which stipulates that people cannot intentionally or recklessly cause serious harm to another. The same principle applies to judicial decisions, for example *R* v *R* (1991), which established that a man could be found guilty of raping his wife.

Breach of legal rules will result in state sanctions and procedures. For example, breach of the criminal law may result in being arrested, charged and prosecuted through the criminal courts. If a person is found guilty, a criminal sanction, such as a fine, may be imposed. With reference to the **Offences Against the Person Act 1861**, for example, breach of s.20 may result in a maximum sentence of 5 years' imprisonment.

Legal rules are created and take effect at a precise time. A precedent is found in the judgement of a case and applies to future cases in lower courts. A piece of legislation/delegated legislation will take effect on a specified commencement date. For example, the **Smoke-free (Premises and Enforcement) Regulations**, made on 13 December 2006, came into force on 1 July 2007.

> **Examiner tip**
> You can cite examples of laws from virtually any part of the specification here.

Characteristics of moral rules

Phil Harris, in *An Introduction to Law*, defines a society's 'code of morality' as a set of beliefs, values, principles and standards of behaviour.

Compliance with moral rules is not required by the state. People may be influenced by family, friends or religion, or may choose for themselves what they consider to be moral or immoral.

Society is pluralistic. What one person considers immoral, another may not. For example, some people may believe that sex before marriage is immoral, while others consider it to be acceptable.

Moral rules develop gradually. They often stem from religious rules made thousands of years ago. Over time, conduct once considered immoral increasingly becomes acceptable. For example, the attitude towards homosexuality continues to change.

Moral rules are enforced informally, usually through social or domestic pressure. A person who repeatedly tells lies or breaks promises, for example, may be shunned or ostracised by friends, family or work colleagues.

Distinctions between legal and moral rules

Many of the distinctions between legal and moral rules emerge through a discussion of their characteristics. It is useful, however, to consider the following distinctions:

- Disagreement regarding the content of a legal rule can be resolved through reference to a precedent or Act of Parliament. This cannot be done with moral rules. Moral rules are not scientific truths and can be argued.
- Legal rules can be changed instantly, whereas moral rules evolve gradually. The legal rules regarding homosexual acts in private between consenting adults were instantly changed when the **Sexual Offences Act 1967** was passed. Society's moral acceptance of homosexuality, however, underwent and continues to undergo gradual change.
- Legal rules are enforced by state sanctions and procedures. Moral rules are enforced through social and domestic pressure, and are sometimes supported not by threats of punishment but by a reminder of the rules' existence, and by an implied appeal to respect them.
- Legal rules can impose strict liability. This can be seen in both criminal and civil law. For example, selling lottery tickets to persons under the age of 16 (*Harrow LBC* v *Shah*, 1999) is a strict liability offence. In civil law, the tort of nuisance is concerned with preventing interference with the enjoyment of proprietary interests. Moral offences, however, can only be committed voluntarily, with full *mens rea*.
- Due to the pluralistic nature of society, the moral codes of the various groups making up British society vary. However, all members of society are obliged to comply with legal rules.

The relationship between legal and moral rules

Any legal system presupposes a certain amount of morality, because if law is not essentially moral there is no easy explanation of the obligation to obey. The relationship between law and morality can perhaps best be described as two intersecting circles. The area inside the intersection represents the coincidence of law and morality, and the areas outside represent areas of divergence.

Knowledge check 1

Who enforces:

(a) legal rules?

(b) moral rules?

Examiner tip

All exam questions will require you to give more than simple definitions. You will be expected to discuss the relationship between law and moral rules. A good answer will identify ways in which they are different, but it will also highlight the overlap between moral and legal rules.

Coincidence of legal and moral rules

Long-established legal rules influenced by moral rules

There are many long-established rules which have a moral connection. These include the laws of murder and theft, which can be traced back to the Ten Commandments.

Public morality may influence judicial change

Criminal law

- The decision in *R* v *R* (1991) was influenced by the moral rule that a husband should not be able to force his wife to have sexual intercourse.
- The decision in *R* v *Brown* (1993) was influenced by the moral rule that holds sadomasochistic activities as being unacceptable, even if consented to.

Contract law

In *Central London Property* v *High Trees House* (1947), Lord Denning created the equitable remedy of promissory estoppel, the basis of which is that people ought not to break their promises.

The law of tort

The decision in *Chadwick* v *British Railways Board* (1967) was influenced by the moral rule that people ought to help others who may be in trouble.

Changes in public morality may influence legislative reform

Many legislative reforms of the 1960s could be said to reflect the 'permissive' moral ideals of that decade. Abortion was legalised by the **Abortion Act 1967**, and the **Sexual Offences Act 1967** legalised homosexual acts in private between consenting adults. The law responded to the continued shift in public morality by reducing the homosexual age of consent, first to 18 in 1994, and then to 16 in 2000. Adoption legislation enacted in 2002 gives gay couples the right to adopt a child, and the **Civil Partnership Act 2004** allows civil registrations that give gay and lesbian couples the same legal entitlements as marriage in areas such as employment, pensions and social security. However, the 2004 Act does not allow religious ceremonies. In the summer of 2012 the government indicated that it intends to move beyond civil partnerships and allow gay marriage.

Another interesting example is the decision in 1986 to ban corporal punishment in state schools. In 1998 the ban was extended to all schools. This reflected the general view that corporal punishment was wrong in principle, yet only a few years earlier it had been widespread in schools and apparently supported by many people.

The law is often slow to respond, as is evident in the reluctance to decriminalise assisted suicide. The conclusions of the British Social Attitudes Survey 2007 found

Examiner tip
An important aspect of the relationship between legal and moral rules is the way in which law changes as moral attitudes change. There are many examples of this that could be considered. Several are discussed in this section. Better answers will provide discussion of a wide range of issues and will show understanding of the complexity of the relationship between law and morality.

that 80% of the population is in favour of assisted suicide if it is helped by a doctor, but as we consider later in this section, the law makers have been reluctant to intervene in this area, conscious no doubt of the strongly held views on both sides of the argument.

Public morality may be influenced by law reform

It can be argued that some legislation is introduced partly with the aim of educating the public to consider certain matters unacceptable, i.e. morally wrong. Discrimination legislation, for example, aims to educate people to regard treating others differently on the grounds of sex, race or disability as wrong.

Law reform may be the product of a campaign to change public morality

In 1949, the Howard League for Penal Reform persuaded the government to appoint a Royal Commission on Capital Punishment. The Howard League then persuaded most members of the Commission to be in favour of the abolition of the death penalty. The government refused to implement the proposals because public opinion considered the death penalty to be morally correct. Subsequently, a pressure group called the National Campaign for the Abolition of Capital Punishment was set up. During the years 1955–57, public opinion was changed by the campaign and the government introduced the necessary legislation to abolish the death penalty.

Reasons for the overlap between legal and moral rules

Legal and moral rules are concerned with imposing certain standards of conduct, without which society would break down. In many of these fundamental standards, law and morality reinforce and supplement each other as part of the fabric of social life. For example, sanctions and remedies imposed by the law reinforce moral disapproval of breaches of legal rules that forbid immoral acts.

Therefore, legal rules do not exist in a vacuum, but, as Harris writes, 'are found side by side with moral codes of greater or less complexity. The relationship of law to moral rules and standards is therefore one of great and abiding importance in every human society, and certainly not least in our own'.

The close link between legal rules and moral rules is also demonstrated by the similarity of normative language that each employs. Both are concerned to lay down rules or 'norms' of conduct for human beings, and this is expressed in both moral and legal language in terms of obligations, duties, or what is right or wrong.

Knowledge check 2

What characteristics do legal and moral rules share?

Divergence of legal and moral rules

Some legal rules appear to have no moral connection

There appears to be little moral justification for the fact that tobacco and alcohol consumption are legal while smoking cannabis is illegal. And is it morally wrong to park on yellow lines or drive on a motorway at 72 miles per hour? There are some arguments, however, against the assertion that such laws have no connection with morals. It may be considered immoral, for example, to park in disabled parking spaces if you are not actually disabled or to partially block roads, making access difficult for emergency services vehicles.

Some moral rules have little or no legal backing

While there is a moral duty to help those who may be in danger, the general position of the law is that there is no liability for an omission to act. For example, the passer-by who fails to rescue someone who is drowning will not be held responsible. However, there are some exceptions in criminal law to this rule, such as when a person creates the danger, as in the case of *R* v *Miller* (1983), or where there is an assumption of responsibility, a special relationship or a contractual duty to act.

The remedy of promissory estoppel, considered earlier, is an exception to the general position of the law that there is no legal requirement to keep a promise. There is, however, a moral duty to do so.

Reasons for the divergence between legal and moral rules

As can be seen from the previous examples, the law often shrinks from pursuing what may be recognised as the path of morality. The reasons for this vary. It may be because the moral attitude is not sufficiently widespread, and the law would not reflect popular morality. It may also be because there are fields of human activity where the law deliberately prefers to abstain from supporting the moral rule because it is felt that the machinery of enforcement is too cumbersome to deal with the moral wrong — more social harm may be created than prevented by legal intervention. This was the reason why the Wolfenden Committee recommended that private homosexual behaviour should be decriminalised.

It was also the reason the legislature delayed making forced marriages illegal. The government was concerned about offending cultural sensitivities. However, as the then minister for racial equality stated: 'The government must respond sensitively to the issues of cultural diversity, but multicultural sensitivity is no excuse for moral blindness.' The **Forced Marriage (Civil Protection) Act 2007** came into effect in November 2008, introducing a civil remedy of a Forced Marriage Protection Order for victims. The government has announced plans to make forced marriage a crime by 2013.

The pluralistic nature of society means coincidence is partial

In England, there is a large population of mixed cultures, races, political ideals and religious followings. This leads to significant divergence of views on a number of moral issues. For example, some people regard abortion as immoral, while others feel it is acceptable for medical reasons only. There is disagreement among those in favour of abortion about the stage of pregnancy at which the procedure is acceptable. In the debates leading up to the **Human Fertilisation and Embryology Act** 190 MPs voted in favour of reducing the current 24-week abortion limit and some MPs favoured a reduction to 12 weeks.

The dispute between some Christians and the gay community over the right of gay couples in civil partnerships to share accommodation in hotels and guest houses illustrates the same problem. In *Bull & Bull v Hall & Preddy* (2012) the Court of Appeal ruled that it was contrary to the **Equality Act (Sexual Orientation Regulations) 2007** to refuse same-sex couples in civil partnerships a double room and commented that in a pluralistic society it was inevitable that from time to time views, beliefs and rights of some would not be compatible with those of others.

It can be argued that there is no public moral consensus on many moral issues. Further examples to consider are *Gillick* v *West Norfolk and Wisbech Area Health Authority* (1986), *Re A (Children)* (2000) and the Diane Pretty, Debbie Purdy and Tony Nicklinson cases, which raised the issue of assisted dying.

Knowledge check 3

What is a pluralistic society?

Natural law theorists

Natural law theorists argue that, in order to be valid, the law must coincide with natural law. Throughout history, many different views have been expressed as to what natural law is.

In the fourth century BC, the Greek philosopher Aristotle based his theory of natural law on the law of nature. He believed that the principles which governed the universe, and which explained how it was structured and how it functioned, could be discovered through observation and the power of human reason.

By the Middle Ages, natural law theorists believed that the natural law was the divine law or the law of God. St Thomas Aquinas, writing in the thirteenth century, expressed the view that the universe was created by God, and that when God created man he enabled him to know the truth. According to Aquinas, man is able to discover the truth of divine law through revelation, for example in the Holy Scriptures, through reflection, and through practical reasoning. Aquinas believed that if human law was at variance with the divine law, it was not legal but rather a corruption of the law.

In more recent times, the influence of the church has arguably declined. Professor Lon Fuller, in his book *Morality of Law* (1964), refers to what he terms the 'inner morality of law'. For Fuller, any legal system is only valid if it conforms to certain procedural requirements, including that law must be understandable and that it must not be retrospective. Many aspects of the English legal system do not comply with

Fuller's requirements. For example, some legislation is not understandable even by the judiciary, and judicial law-making is retrospective. While the decision in *R* v *R* (1991) was welcomed because it reflected public morality, it was retrospective in effect. In *R* v *Crooks* (2004), the Court of Appeal upheld the conviction (in 2002) of the defendant, who had had sexual intercourse with his wife without her consent in 1970, 21 years before such behaviour was made a criminal offence.

While it can be seen that views expressed as to what natural law is have varied, there is nevertheless a common thread. As Lord Lloyd of Hampstead points out in *Introduction to Jurisprudence*: 'What has remained constant is an assertion that there are principles of natural law...the essence of natural law may be said to lie in the constant assertion that there are objective moral principles which depend upon the nature of the universe and which can be discovered by reason.'

Positivists

Jeremy Bentham

Jeremy Bentham (1748–1832) rejected natural law theories as being 'nonsense upon stilts'. His key criticisms were that natural law was based upon unprovable principles, and that natural law theorists confused legal issues with moral issues. For Bentham, the validity of a law did not depend on whether it was good or bad. What the law is and what the law ought to be should be treated as different issues. Bentham was primarily concerned with the promotion of the utility principle, i.e. the greatest happiness for the greatest number. However, a law not promoting this principle would not automatically be adjudged to be invalid.

John Austin

John Austin (1790–1859) is credited with formulating the first coherent theory of positivism. He rejected the principle of natural law, whereby validity of law is dependent upon it not being in conflict with a 'higher law', be it natural or divine. For Austin, a law may be valid irrespective of its moral content. He defined law in terms of a command from a sovereign, whom the bulk of society is in the habit of obeying, enforced by a sanction. The origins of the command theory can be traced to Bentham and to Hobbes (1588–1679).

H. L. A. Hart

Professor Hart, in his book *The Concept of Law* (1963), also subscribes to the positivist view, while being critical of some aspects of Austin's command theory.

The Hart–Devlin debate

The issue of how far law and morals should coincide was widely discussed in the late 1950s, when there was public concern about an apparent decline in sexual morality. This became known as the Hart–Devlin debate, not to be confused with the Hart–Fuller debate, which was concerned with the validity of legal rules that conflict with moral rules. The Hart–Devlin debate was concerned with the extent to which the law should enforce moral rules.

Statements reflecting the pluralistic nature of society can be found in the debates surrounding the legal reforms of the 1960s. The **Sexual Offences Act 1967**, which legalised homosexuality, was introduced following recommendations made by the Wolfenden Committee in its 1957 report. Two years after the publication of the Wolfenden Report, Lord Devlin, in his book, *The Enforcement of Morals*, set out his criticisms of the Wolfenden recommendations. In 1962, Professor Hart set out his arguments against Devlin's views in his book, *Law, Liberty and Morality*.

Professor Hart drew on the work of John Stuart Mill who, in his essay 'On liberty' (1859), stated: 'The only part of the conduct of anyone, for which he is amenable to society, is that which concerns others. In the part which merely concerns himself, his independence, is of right, absolute. Over himself, over his own body and mind, the individual is sovereign.' John Stuart Mill and Professor Hart put forward the view that the minority should not be made to conform to the will of the majority when in private, as this would amount to tyranny and be immoral. They thus recognised the pluralistic nature of society.

Professor Hart argued that using law to enforce moral values was unnecessary, undesirable and morally unacceptable: unnecessary because society was capable of containing many moral standpoints without disintegrating; undesirable because it would freeze morality at a particular point; and morally unacceptable because it infringes the freedom of the individual. He also pointed out that objections to unusual behaviour are often prompted by ignorance, prejudice and misunderstanding.

Knowledge check 4

What view did Mill and Hart have about the legal enforcement of morals?

Sir James Stephen, a leading criminal judge in the late nineteenth century, disagreed with Mill. In his work *Liberty, Equality, Fraternity* (1874) he stated:

> I think that the attempt to distinguish between self-regarding acts and acts which regard others is like an attempt to distinguish between acts which happen in time and acts which happen in space. Every act happens at some time and in some space, and, in like manner, every act that we do either does or may affect both ourselves and others. I therefore think that the distinction is altogether fallacious and unfounded.

He went on to say: 'There are acts of wickedness so gross and outrageous that they must be punished at any cost to the offender.' Stephen's view was that the prevention of immoral behaviour was an end in itself.

Lord Devlin's views are more in line with those of Sir James Stephen. While Devlin believed that individual privacy should be respected, he stated: 'History shows that the loosening of moral bonds is often the first stage of disintegration...suppression of vice is as much the law's business as the suppression of subversive activities.' He believed that society shared a common morality and that the law should intervene to punish acts which offend that shared morality, whether done in public or private. Failure to intervene would result in the disintegration of society. He argued that individual liberty could only flourish in a stable society; disintegration of society through lack of a shared morality would, therefore, threaten individual freedom.

Knowledge check 5

What view did Stephen and Devlin have about the legal enforcement of morals?

Examiner tip

Discussion of the Hart–Devlin debate is central to any consideration of what the relationship between law and morality should be. Better students will demonstrate detailed knowledge of the views of both Professor Hart and Lord Devlin, and will be able to explain how the debate has influenced the law in recent years.

Knowledge check 6

How does the decision in ADT v UK (2000) reflect the Mill–Hart approach?

The influence of Mill–Hart

Sir John Wolfenden followed the views of Mill and Hart, recognising the pluralistic nature of society and the importance of individual liberty. The resulting legislation, the **Sexual Offences Act 1967**, legalising homosexuality, was thus influenced by the views of Mill and Hart. Their views were also reflected in other reforming legislation of that period such as the Obscene Publications Act 1968 and the Divorce Law Reform Act 1969.

The majority of the House of Lords in *Gillick* v *Norfolk and Wisbech Area Health Authority* (1986) also adopted the Mill–Hart approach. They held that it was legal for doctors to offer contraceptive advice and treatment to girls under the age of 16 without parental consent, provided they were satisfied that the girls had sufficient understanding of the issues involved. Lord Scarman said that 'parental rights are derived from parental duty' and that the 'dwindling right' of a parent as the child grows older 'yields to the child's right to make his own decision when he reaches a sufficient understanding and intelligence to be capable of making up his own mind on the matter requiring decision'.

More recently, the European Court of Human Rights was influenced by the Mill–Hart approach in *ADT* v *UK* (2000). The European Court of Human Rights ruled that the conviction of a man who engaged in non-violent consensual homosexual acts in private with up to four other men was a violation of Article 8 — the right to respect for private life.

The influence of Stephen–Devlin

The dissenting judgements of Lords Brandon and Templeman in *Gillick* v *Norfolk and Wisbech Area Health Authority* (1986) reflected concerns over the wider social implications. Lord Brandon's dissent was based largely on the question of public policy and his concern for the criminal aspect in terms of underage sex. Lord Templeman ignored case law and produced an opinion, the most memorable line of which is: 'There are many things which a girl under 16 needs to practise but sex is not one of them.' These views were an echo of Lord Devlin's concern about social disintegration.

The influence of Stephen and Devlin can be seen in a number of other judicial decisions. In *Shaw* v *DPP* (1962), the Ladies' Directory case, the House of Lords ruled that a publication advertising the services of prostitutes was a conspiracy to corrupt public morals. Viscount Simmonds argued: 'In the sphere of criminal law I entertain no doubt that there remains in the courts a residual power to enforce the supreme and fundamental purpose of the law, to conserve not only the safety and order, but also the moral welfare of the state.' In *R* v *Gibson* (1990) an artist exhibited earrings made from freeze-dried foetuses of 3–4 months' gestation. A conviction for the common law offence of outraging public decency was upheld. These cases show that there is still judicial support for the Devlin viewpoint that some acts are intrinsically immoral, regardless of whether they harm others.

Perhaps the most significant decisions are those of the House of Lords in *R* v *Brown* (1993) and the European Court of Human Rights (ECtHR) in *Laskey, Brown and Jaggard* v *United Kingdom* (1997). In the House of Lords case, the question was whether the defence of consent could be used in respect of sadomasochistic acts. The people involved were consenting adults and none of the activities was conducted in public or had resulted in the need for medical treatment. The activities concerned included whipping, caning, branding and nailing their genitals to pieces of wood. The House of Lords held that the defence of consent could not be applied to such practices and that such behaviour was not to be encouraged by relaxation of the law. When the defendants took their case to the ECtHR they lost on the basis that there was no breach of Article 8, as infringement of the right to respect for private life was justified by the need to protect health or morals. This approach was followed in *R* v *Emmett* (1999). A woman consented to her partner covering her head with a plastic bag and tying it tightly at the neck, and to him pouring lighter fuel on her breasts and setting them alight. The court held her consent did not provide a defence to her partner.

Knowledge check 7

Which two cases seem to illustrate the Devlin view that some acts are intrinsically immoral, regardless of whether they harm others?

The continuing relevance of the debate

The development of the law in relation to homosexual couples continues to reflect the Mill–Hart view. Under the **Equality Act (Sexual Orientation Regulations) 2007** homosexual people cannot be treated differently from anyone else when providing goods and services. Under these regulations people in civil partnerships (introduced in 2005) must be treated the same as heterosexual married couples. The Court of Appeal decision in *Bull & Bull* v *Hall & Preddy* (2012), which upheld the entitlement of gay couples in civil partnerships to shared accommodation in hotels and guest houses, reflects the influence of Mill and Hart.

Adoption is a service also covered by the Equality Act. There was considerable opposition from Catholic adoption agencies which wanted to gain exemption from the regulations. In April 2011 the Charity Tribunal rejected an appeal by Catholic Care which had sought to restrict its adoption service to heterosexual couples. Catholic Care had claimed it would give up its adoption service rather than comply with the regulations. It would appear that the law in this respect reflects the Mill–Hart view.

However, on the issue of gay adoption, as with gay marriage, there are split views as to whether harm to others will result. Groups like Stonewall argue that it is clearly in the best interest of children in care to encourage as wide a pool of potential adopters as possible, while the Roman Catholic Church contends that placing children with same-sex couples would create obstacles to the normal development of those children.

Proposals by the coalition government to introduce legislation lifting the ban on same-sex marriage in civil ceremonies also reflected the Mill–Hart approach. A consultation document was issued in March 2012 concerning lifting the ban on same-sex marriage in civil ceremonies. However, considerable reaction from conservative MPs and some government ministers appears to have influenced the omission of same-sex marriage from the 2012 Queen's speech and an announcement that the prime minister will allow a free vote when the matter is debated in Parliament.

Examiner tip

This is often the weakest part of many student answers. A good answer will be able to refer to recent examples which illustrate the continuing relevance of the debate. A number of issues are discussed in this section, but it is important to look out for other issues which may arise after publication of this book and to update your notes with any developments which may affect existing issues.

In contrast the legislation relating to assisted suicide seems to reflect the Devlin view. There has been no decriminalisation of assisted suicide in the UK despite a considerable shift in public opinion. Assisted suicide is punishable by a maximum of 14 years' imprisonment.

According to the British Social Attitudes Survey 2007, 80% of the public are in favour of giving terminally ill patients the right to die with the help of a doctor. But in May 2006 the House of Lords rejected Lord Joffe's **Assisted Dying Bill** which proposed that doctors should be allowed to prescribe a lethal dose of medication. The bill generated considerable debate between supporters of the right to die and supporters of better palliative care. The debate has been reignited by the 2012 Tony Nicklinson case.

Britain's major faith groups argue that assisted suicide and euthanasia undermine respect for life, and the British Medical Association is opposed to any change to the law.

The authorities appear reluctant to come down on one side or the other. There have been no prosecutions so far of relatives of more than 100 UK citizens who have gone to Switzerland to die. However, in February 2009 the Court of Appeal in a case brought by **Debbie Purdy** ruled that relatives could not be given a guarantee that they would not be prosecuted. This confirmed the decision of the House of Lords and the European Court of Human Rights in the **Dianne Pretty** case brought in 2001. In January 2010 **Kay Gilderdale** was tried for attempted murder after she admitted helping her daughter to die by handing her two syringes of morphine. The jury acquitted her and the CPS was criticised for prosecuting her for this when she had already pleaded guilty to assisted suicide.

Knowledge check 8

Why is it suggested that the law on assisted suicide seems to reflect the Stephen–Devlin view?

So although the law reflects the Devlin view, it is clear that there is a reluctance to enforce the law and a growing recognition that there is much public sympathy for relatives who help loved ones to die. The conditional discharge that Kay Gilderdale received for assisted suicide is an indication perhaps of the approach that is likely to be adopted in the future.

Conclusion

One of the difficulties for the law is not only that society is pluralistic, but also that views are sometimes passionately held, allowing little scope for compromise. In general terms, it could be argued that a large section of society has come to adopt the view taken by Professor Hart, and inevitably this has been reflected in both legislative changes and judicial decisions. On the other hand, significant groups remain opposed to what they perceive as a dangerous weakening of the moral basis of law.

Characteristics of legal rules:

- Salmond — principles applied by state; Austin — command theory
- compliance compulsory
- enforced by state
- created at precise time

Characteristics of moral rules:

- Harris — beliefs, values, principles, standards of behaviour
- compliance not required by state
- society pluralistic, e.g. abortion
- develop gradually, e.g. attitudes to homosexuals
- enforced informally

Distinctions between legal and moral rules:

- Laws exist; moral rules are not scientific truths.
- Laws made instantly; moral rules evolve.
- Enforcement — law by state, moral rules informal.
- Laws can impose strict liability; moral rules cannot.
- Moral codes vary; laws same for everybody.

Relationship between legal and moral rules: intersecting circles.

Coincidence of legal and moral rules:

- Long-established laws influenced by moral rules, e.g. murder, theft.
- Public morality influences judiciary, e.g. R v R (1991).
- Public morality influences legislature, e.g. Civil Partnership Act 2004.
- Law influences public morality, e.g. discrimination.
- Law follows campaign to change public morality.
- Shared characteristics — impose standards, normative language, preserve society.

Divergence of legal and moral rules:

- laws with no moral connection, e.g. parking, speeding
- moral rules with little/no legal backing, e.g. rescuers

- legislature hesitant when moral views insufficiently widespread, enforcement problems, cultural sensitivities, e.g. forced marriage
- coincidence partial in pluralistic society, e.g. abortion

Natural law theorists:

- validity of law dependent on compliance with natural law
- Aristotle — law of nature; Aquinas — law of God; Lon Fuller — procedural requirements
- common thread — Lord Lloyd — objective moral principles dependent on nature of universe, discoverable by reason

Positivists:

- Bentham — validity of law not dependent on whether good or bad, is/ought distinction
- Austin — law valid irrespective of moral content, command theory
- Hart — positivist

Hart/Devlin debate:

- Mill–Hart — harm to others theory, 'In the part which merely concerns himself, his independence, is of right, absolute'
- Stephen — public/private distinction unfounded
- Devlin — 'the loosening of moral bonds is often the first stage of disintegration', suppression of vice responsibility of law
- influence of Mill–Hart: Sexual Offences Act 1967, Gillick, ADT v UK (2000)
- influence of Stephen–Devlin: Gillick dissenting judgements, Shaw v DPP, R v Gibson (1990), R v Brown (1993), Laskey, Brown and Jaggard v UK (1997), R v Emmett (1999)

Continuing relevance of the debate:

- Mill–Hart — Bull & Bull v Hall & Preddy (2012), adoption available to homosexual couples, proposal to legalise same-sex marriage
- Stephen–Devlin — assisted suicide not decriminalised, but no prosecutions regarding Switzerland, reluctance to punish, e.g. Kay Gilderdale conditional discharge

Law and justice

The meaning of 'justice'

'Justice' has many meanings. The definition given in the *Oxford English Dictionary* is 'just conduct; fairness', and this is the common understanding of the word. The definition of 'just' is 'acting or done in accordance with what is morally right or proper'. The definition of 'fair' is 'free from discrimination, dishonesty...in conformity with rules or standards'. Lord Lloyd emphasises the difficulty in defining justice precisely: 'Justice, whatever its precise meaning may be, is itself a moral value, that is one of the aims or purposes which man sets himself in order to attain the good life.' It would appear that conceptions of justice vary from age to age, and person to person, and according to existing economic relations.

Perelman recognised that justice has several meanings. In his book, *De La Justice* (1945), he set out six possible meanings of justice:

(1) 'To each according to his works' (rewards are based on contribution)

(2) 'To each according to his needs' (people receive what they need)

(3) 'To each according to his merits' (people get what they deserve)

(4) 'To each according to his rank' (people may enjoy privileges according to status)

(5) 'To each according to his legal entitlement' (people receive what the law says they should)

(6) 'To each equally' (all people receive the same)

While recognising that justice may have several meanings, Perelman believed that once the type of justice subscribed to by a society was identified, then all individuals had to be treated the same. He subscribed to the theory of formal justice.

Justice, according to the law, can be formal, substantive, distributive or corrective, or any combination of these types:
- Formal justice, often referred to as procedural justice, requires equality of treatment in accordance with the classification laid down by rules.
- Substantive justice is concerned with whether rules are just.
- Distributive justice is concerned with the fair allocation of benefits and burdens within society.
- Corrective justice requires the righting of wrongs through fair remedy or punishment.

Theories of justice

There are numerous theories of justice. It is important to be able to explain and evaluate these theories and their relationships with each other, and to understand their application to modern society.

Examiner tip

Most exam questions require you to explain in theory what justice is, and then to explain how far in practice justice is achieved. However, a common fault is to define justice well and to give examples of justice in operation, but not to link these two parts.

Examiner tip

It is a good idea to begin by defining justice and exploring some of the various meanings and types of justice that have been suggested. Refer if you can to the individuals who suggested these meanings.

Aristotle

The Greek philosopher Aristotle introduced the principles of distributive justice and corrective justice:

- The principle of distributive justice requires that the allocation of assets in society should be proportional to a person's claim on them. He argued that this did not necessarily mean equal shares.
- The principle of corrective justice requires that where distributive justice is disturbed by wrongdoing, there should be a means of restoring the original position. Corrective justice operates in English law through the system of state sanctions imposed in criminal law and remedies provided to the victim in civil law. It also operates through the appeals system and this can be seen particularly in the miscarriage of justice cases.

Natural law theorists

Aquinas's **natural law theory** assumes that if higher law is followed, the result will be justice. An unjust law might be contrary to human good or against the higher law derived from God. A law which goes against this God-derived law will always be 'unjust' and should not be obeyed. Some Roman Catholics today would argue that this applies to laws legalising abortion. Members of many faith groups would find it difficult to obey laws that compelled them to break what they regard as fundamental principles. Some Christians in the UK argue that recent legislation has made it difficult for them to share their faith with others and nurses, for example, have been disciplined for offering to pray with patients.

In more recent times, the influence of the church has declined, and natural law theorists have based their ideas on different kinds of fundamentals. **Professor Lon Fuller**, in his book, *Morality of Law*, published in 1963, refers to what he terms the 'inner morality of law'. For Fuller, a legal system is only just and therefore valid if it conforms to eight procedural requirements.

The Human Rights Act would suggest that there is a close connection between the law and the natural law theorists' concept of justice, because it incorporates into English law the European Convention on Human Rights which sets out 'fundamental' rights, such as the right to life, freedom of expression and freedom from torture. Natural law theorists would not support the Law Lords' decision in the Debbie Purdy case (2009) because it does not uphold the sanctity of human life.

Utilitarianism

The **theory of utilitarianism** was developed by Jeremy Bentham. The aim of utilitarianism is to maximise human happiness by increasing pleasure and diminishing pain. For the utilitarian, justice is concerned with promoting 'the greatest happiness of the greatest number'. The sum of human happiness is assessed by numerical means and each person's happiness is equal in value.

Utilitarianism is a secular theory. It has been influential in legal reform and appears to be based on democratic principles. Utilitarian principles arguably underpin English law because Parliament, the sovereign law maker, is elected. The legislative process

Knowledge check 9

Who developed the theory of utilitarianism?

is democratic and should ensure that legislation is created only if it pleases the majority. However, it can be argued that the population plays a small part in statute creation because MPs vote along party lines and the government only has to answer to the electorate every 5 years in an election.

Utilitarianism can be criticised for being difficult to apply in practice: it is questionable whether happiness can be directly or precisely measured. Another criticism is that utilitarianism is concerned with the consequences of an act and not the means by which it is achieved. Thus, torture may justify the end result of obtaining information. Individuals are not regarded as important and the complete misery of a few is justified if it increases the happiness of the many.

Positivism

John Austin developed the ideas of Bentham. Like Bentham, Austin also rejected the principle of natural law. For Austin, a law may be valid irrespective of its moral content or whether it delivers justice. Professor Hart in *The Concept of Law* (1963) also subscribes to the positivist view. He argues that it is possible to administer unjust laws in a just manner and vice versa.

John Rawls

John Rawls in *A Theory of Justice* (1971) sets out justice as fairness. In order to avoid the situation whereby people exploit social and natural circumstances to their own advantage, Rawls places people in the original position behind a 'veil of ignorance', whereby 'the parties do not know certain kinds of particular facts. First of all, no one knows his place in society, his class position or social status; nor does he know his fortune in the distribution of natural assets and abilities, his intelligence and strength and the like'. Furthermore, people behind the veil of ignorance do not know what they will value as good or bad, or what economic or political situation, level of civilisation and culture are prevalent in their society. He argues that 'the idea of the original position is to set up a fair procedure so that any principles agreed to will be just'. According to Rawls, two principles would be chosen from these circumstances: 'First: each person is to have an equal right to the most extensive basic liberty compatible with a similar liberty for others. Second: social and economic inequalities are to be arranged so that they are both (a) reasonably expected to be to everyone's advantage, and (b) attached to positions and offices open to all.'

Rawls's theory of justice is reflected in both English law and the European Convention on Human Rights. Rawls subscribes to liberalism, which is primarily concerned with freedom and the autonomy of individuals. The Human Rights Act and the European Convention on Human Rights reflect this in that they ensure individuals are given the positive rights Rawls regards as important, including freedom of speech and assembly and freedom from arbitrary arrest and seizure. However, the derogation clauses depart from Rawls's theory, allowing for a denial of rights, for example 'in the interests of national security, public safety or the economic well-being of the country, for the prevention of disorder or crime, for the protection of health or morals, or for the protection of the rights and freedoms of others' (Article 8). Only the last point arguably reflects Rawls's theory, in that individual liberty can be limited if it will result in greater liberty overall.

Rawls rejects the notion of utility. He believes that justice is achieved through rules which create inequality only if that inequality is of benefit to all, not merely to the greatest number. Furthermore, the equal right to liberty cannot be denied in favour of greater social or economic advantages. Like Aristotle, Rawls supports the idea of distributive justice and it is clear that the English legal system is based on the idea of distributive justice in that the law does allocate benefits and burdens through rights and duties, for example under the Human Rights Act and also through state funding of access to the justice system, although this is in decline.

Knowledge check 10

How does the Human Rights Act not support Rawls's theory?

Marxism

Karl Marx, like Rawls, subscribed to an ideal of justice rather than to an actual existing system. For Marx, the ideal society meant 'From each according to his ability, to each according to his needs'. He argued that justice cannot be achieved until the ideal society is in place, for any other society is defective and justice therein impossible. However, Marx also propounded the view that 'Once the new productive arrangements appear, there will be no need for principles of justice for production or distribution.' Justice for Marx would be the existence of his ideal society and there would apparently be no need for a law to conform to.

Such sentiments were also expressed by eighteenth-century theorist **David Hume**: 'If every man had a tender regard for another, or if nature supplied abundantly all our wants and desires...the jealousy of interest, which justice supposes, could no longer have place. Increase to a sufficient degree the benevolence of men, or the bounty of nature, and you render justice useless.' It is clear that Britain does not correspond to the ideal society as envisaged by either Hume or Marx.

Robert Nozick and the minimal state

Nozick rejected the distributive theories of justice of Rawls and Marx and instead developed the **entitlement theory** of justice, according to which goods arise already encumbered with ownership. He maintained that individuals have natural rights to the enjoyment of life, health, liberty and possessions, free from interference by others. Rather than being concerned with equality, the entitlement theory stipulates that the state should only intervene to protect natural rights: inequalities are a fact of life. It holds that the state should play a minimum role and is not justified in diminishing or increasing the natural rights which an individual possesses. Redistribution of individuals' rights is not justified for any social purpose. Legal systems such as that operating in the UK, which go further than merely enforcing natural rights, do not comply with Nozick's theory of justice.

The extent to which justice is achieved

The extent to which English law achieves justice varies according to which theory of justice is ascribed to. Justice is not achieved according to Nozick and Marx, but to a varying extent justice is achieved according to the other theories.

Examiner tip

In questioning whether the English law complies with the requirements of formal and substantive justice, you can use examples of rules, institutions and processes from many parts of the specification. You can then relate these examples to the meanings and theories of justice and examine them in order to assess how successful they are in achieving justice.

Natural justice and the rule of law

It would be reasonable to claim that if a legal system is to be based on justice, it must incorporate the principles of natural justice and the rule of law.

Phil Harris, in *An Introduction to Law*, argues that the idea of natural justice 'has no mysterious or magical meaning: it simply refers to a duty to act fairly'. This is based on two requirements: that each party should have the opportunity to be heard and that no one should be judge in his or her own cause. This principle can be seen operating in *R v Bow Street Metropolitan Stipendiary Magistrates, ex parte Pinochet* (1999), in which the House of Lords decided that General Pinochet, the former dictator of Chile, should be extradited to Spain to face serious charges of human rights abuse. When it was revealed that Lord Hoffman, one of the Law Lords who heard the case, had links with Amnesty International, a human rights organisation involved in the proceedings, the House of Lords annulled the decision and reheard the case without Lord Hoffman.

The theory of the rule of law as outlined by Dicey in the nineteenth century is that 'no person is punishable except for a distinct breach of the law established in the courts' and also that no man is 'above the law, but that every man, whatever his rank, is subject to the ordinary law of the realm'.

Judicial review

One of the ways in which the rule of law is guaranteed is by having an independent judiciary able to review the decisions of politicians and public officials.

The process of judicial review examines whether the body or individual in question was within their rights in making the decision. It is a means of formal justice. If a decision is *ultra vires*, it can be quashed. Procedural *ultra vires* arises where proper procedures have not been followed. Substantive *ultra vires* arises where the content of the decision was outside the power of the body that made it.

An example of procedural *ultra vires* was the government's decision to build a third runway at Heathrow. In March 2010 the High Court agreed with a coalition of several bodies, including residents, local authorities, Greenpeace and the Campaign to Protect Rural England, that the consultation carried out by the government into a third runway at Heathrow had not taken account of the latest evidence.

The passing of the **Human Rights Act 1998** has enabled judges to review even primary legislation to determine whether it complies with the European Convention on Human Rights. In *A and Others v Secretary of State for the Home Department* (2004), the House of Lords took the view that the detention of foreign nationals without trial under s.21 of the **Anti-Terrorism, Crime and Security Act 2001** was not compatible with article 14 even though the government argued that they were a threat to national security.

Judicial independence

Judicial independence is fundamental to the rule of natural justice that no one should be a judge in his or her own cause — *nemo judex in causa sua*. An aspect of judicial

Knowledge check 11

How does the decision in *A and Others v Secretary of State for the Home Department* (2004) confirm an element of the rule of law?

Examiner tip

One approach to a question on the achievement of justice is to suggest that in terms of the fundamental principles substantive justice is achieved in the UK because of the operation of the rule of law, natural justice and judicial review. Your answer might then go on to consider problems with the application of these principles, which have sometimes led to a lack of procedural justice.

independence is that judges should be independent from the case. The example of the Pinochet case has already been mentioned.

Similarly, in *Morrison* v *AWG Group Ltd and another* (2006), the Court of Appeal held that a High Court judge should have stood down from hearing the case. He acknowledged that he had known a witness for some 30 years, and consequently that witness was replaced. The judge then heard the case. Lord Justice Mummery stated that in such situations judges should stand down to avoid any perception of bias, however unjustified such a perception might be.

Knowledge check 12

How do the cases of Pinochet and *Morrison* v *AWG Group Ltd and another* (2006) illustrate natural justice?

Access to justice

Government funding for legal cases was introduced by the **Legal Aid Act 1949**, with the aim of providing the means for everyone to have access to justice, rather than only those who could afford it. The system was means tested and demand-led so that all those who applied would receive funding, provided they fell within the eligibility criteria. When the system was first introduced, approximately 80% of the population was eligible for some government funding; however by 2009, according to Ministry of Justice figures, eligibility had reduced to 29%. **The Legal Aid (Sentencing and Punishment of Offenders) Act 2012** will lower eligibility further. Several types of action have been removed from legal funding including most housing, welfare, medical negligence, employment, debt and immigration cases. In addition, the financial limit of claims for which legal funding is available to those on low income for advice has been increased from £5,000 to £10,000 with a view to increasing it in future years to £15,000. The controversy surrounding the passing of the Act is reflected in the 14 defeats it suffered in the Lords. Perhaps the most contentious issue on which the government yielded to pressure was the removal of a clause which allowed for means testing of legal advice given to suspects in the police station. The clause was widely and fiercely opposed on the basis that it would undermine the right of detainees to free advice.

The rules regarding government funding suggest that formal justice is denied. The law in general cannot be applied impartially if certain sections of society are denied access to it or are denied adequate legal representation. It can also be argued that such rules are substantially unjust because they have the effect of denying equal access. The cutting of funding also conflicts with the theories of distributive and corrective justice as argued by Aristotle and Rawls.

The criminal justice system

The miscarriage of justice cases in the 1980s and 1990s, such as the Guildford Four, Judith Ward, the Maguires and the Birmingham Six, raised questions about the way the criminal justice system was operating and suggested that in their eagerness to get convictions, the police had compromised some of the principles of formal justice. In particular, there were concerns about confessions and the treatment of the defendants while they were in custody and also about the reliability of forensic evidence.

Arguably, however, the system did eventually deliver justice, because the appeal system led to the convictions in all these IRA cases, and in others, such as the

Tottenham Three and the Bridgewater Four, being quashed and compensation being paid, thus providing corrective justice.

One of the problems with achieving procedural justice is that it is heavily dependent on the integrity of those responsible for the investigation and prosecution of crime. In particular, there is often a reluctance to disclose evidence which might weaken the prosecution case. This happened for example when both **Sally Clark** and **Angela Cannings** were convicted of murder following the cot deaths of their babies. In these cases the miscarriage was caused by the evidence given by an expert witness, Professor Sir Roy Meadow. He was an eminent paediatrician and he had a theory that where there were multiple cot deaths in the same family the chances of it not being murder were only one in 73 million. In fact his calculations were incorrect, but both women, despite there being no other evidence, were convicted of murder. Their convictions were eventually quashed and Sir Roy Meadow discredited.

In May 2012 **Sam Hallam** was freed after serving 7 years for murder. The Court of Appeal, which had heard that photographs on Mr Hallam's mobile phone could have helped his defence case, ruled his conviction was 'unsafe'. The Court also decided that there was a failure by police to investigate his alibi, and witnesses who put him at the scene of the murder were unreliable.

Justice in this case was achieved due to the case being referred to the Court of Appeal by the **Criminal Cases Review Commission (CCRC)**, an independent body with the responsibility for investigating potential miscarriages of justice. When delivering judgement Lady Justice Hallett said she was 'indebted to the CCRC'. Set up in 1997 following several high-profile miscarriage of justice cases, it has been responsible for identifying and bringing forward a number of appeals, including those by Barry George, Sally Clark and Sion Jenkins, which eventually led to the convictions being quashed.

But this body is itself now under threat from cuts to government funding and there is growing concern among rank and file lawyers and the families of people in prison that the CCRC is finding it increasingly difficult to investigate all the cases where there might have been a miscarriage of justice.

Justice for victims?

The Stephen Lawrence case demonstrates that there can also be concerns about whether the institutions of the state operate fairly in the interests of all those affected by crime. Victims, unlike defendants, do not get a second chance. The suspects were acquitted and a private prosecution was also unsuccessful. The acquittals in this case were influential in the 'double jeopardy' rule being relaxed. The **Criminal Justice Act 2003 (CJA)** allows for people acquitted of certain serious offences to be retried, provided both the DPP and the Court of Appeal are satisfied that there is 'new and compelling evidence' and that it is in the interests of justice to have a retrial. In the Stephen Lawrence case police investigations continued and in December 2011 two men were convicted of the murder of Stephen Lawrence, including one man (Gary Dobson) who had previously been acquitted of the murder and was tried again because of 'new and compelling evidence'. However, the Lawrence family feel that

Knowledge check 13

What type of justice does the appeals process provide?

they have still not received justice because three people accused of the murder are still at large.

The relevant clauses of the **Criminal Justice Act 2003** became law in April 2005 and Joshua Rozenberg, writing in the *Daily Telegraph,* suggested that there might be as many as 35 murder cases that could be retried as a result of the change in the law. The first such case concerned **William Dunlop** who had been acquitted of the murder of his girlfriend in 1989. However, while in prison for another offence he told a prison officer that he had murdered her. As soon as the Criminal Justice Act reforms came into effect prosecutors applied for a retrial and he pleaded guilty to murder in 2006.

The case of Damilola Taylor also focused on the sense of frustration felt by the families of victims when there are unsuccessful prosecutions. The response of the press to the acquittal of the defendants in the initial case, suggested in the words of the *Daily Mirror*, was that this was 'another murdered black boy betrayed by British justice'. But David Pannick, in an article in *The Times* (7 May, 2002), pointed out that justice can be served when defendants are acquitted because the jury is not satisfied of guilt beyond reasonable doubt. The police persevered with the investigation and in 2006 two brothers were convicted of manslaughter. Vital leads connecting the brothers to the offence were originally missed by investigators and a forensic laboratory, but were later picked up by a private science laboratory.

Victims of crime may also seek justice through the civil system. For example, all criminal assaults are also actionable torts, and victims can thus seek compensation from the attacker. In most cases, there is little point as the defendant does not have sufficient assets, but the mechanism did work in *A v Hoare and Others* (2008). In 1989, the defendant was convicted of raping the claimant and received a life sentence. In 2004, having been released on licence, he won £7 million on the National Lottery. The House of Lords held that, in the circumstances, the claimant's action for damages was not barred by the **Limitation Act 1980**.

When a defendant has been acquitted, victims can bring an action in the civil courts. The standard of proof is lower in civil courts and it is easier to prove something on a balance of probabilities. An example is the decision of the High Court in December 2005 in which property baron Nicholas van Hoogstraten was held responsible for the murder of a business rival. Sometimes such a civil ruling prompts a new investigation, resulting in a successful criminal prosecution. An example is the Lynn Siddons case. In 1991, the High Court ruled that Michael Brookes had killed the 16-year-old in 1978. The original police case was found to have been bungled and a fresh investigation took place. In 1996, he was convicted of the murder.

Juries and the achievement of justice

Juries illustrate the difficulty in achieving corrective justice. Juries are arguably fundamental in ensuring justice. Lord Devlin said 'they are the lamp that shows that freedom lives' and they allow ordinary people to exercise independent justice without fear of state interference as illustrated by the jury decision in *Ponting*.

However, as the Roskill Commission said, juries may have difficulty understanding complex fraud cases and may acquit or convict someone wrongly, creating injustice for the victim or defendant. A report for the Ministry of Justice in 2010 found that two out of three jurors do not fully understand the legal directions given to them by judges when they retire to consider their verdicts.

Jury nobbling with bribes or threats could also affect jury decisions and make them unfair. As a result, the **Criminal Justice Act 2003** allows trial by a judge without a jury if there is a real danger of jury nobbling. In *Twomey* (2010) the defendants were convicted of serious offences after a trial without a jury after three previous jury trials — the last one having been abandoned due to jury nobbling.

There is also an increasing risk that jurors will be able to find out information about the defendant from the internet, even though this is something they are expressly forbidden to do. A report for the Ministry of Justice in February 2010 found that 12% of jurors in high-profile cases admitted researching on the internet, and a further 26% said they had come across media reports online during the trial.

In January 2012, **Theodora Dallas**, a juror who researched a defendant's past on the internet and shared the information with fellow jury members, was jailed for 6 months for contempt of court. Modern technology also enables jurors to communicate with other people during the trial. In June 2011, **Joanne Fraill** was given an 8-month jail term after becoming the first juror to be prosecuted for contempt of court for using the internet.

However, the conclusions of the **Thomas Report** in 2010 suggest that juries seem remarkably free from racial prejudice at least. They found that conviction rates for white and Asian defendants were identical and those for black defendants only slightly higher and that all white juries did not discriminate against ethnic minority defendants. Their research also found that even before the introduction of the new rules on selection: 'serving jurors were remarkably representative of the local community in terms of: ethnicity, gender, income, occupation, religion and age' and that there 'was no significant under-representation of black and minority ethnic groups'.

Substantive criminal law: intoxication

This defence is useful in the context of justice because it illustrates the difficulty the law has in striking a balance which is fair to both victim and defendant. Currently, involuntary intoxication is a defence to specific but not basic intent crimes. Formal justice requires consistency in the way rules operate and yet we treat basic and specific intent in different ways. Furthermore, there is potential injustice in that someone can be found guilty even though he or she is clearly unable to form the *mens rea* for even a basic intent crime.

This problem was recognised by the House of Lords in *DPP* v *Majewski* (1977), but it firmly resisted the idea that voluntary intoxication should become a general defence, because this would be socially undesirable. Lord Salmon argued that one important aspect of individual liberty was protection against physical violence, and because the intoxication rule helped to achieve this 'the rule works without imperilling justice'.

Knowledge check 14

Which serious criminal case was decided without a jury because of the problem of jury nobbling?

Examiner tip

Substantive law offers a range of examples which might illustrate the achievement of justice. Some are mentioned here, but many others could be used.

Substantive law: tort

It is useful to consider the strict liability torts of nuisance and *Rylands* v *Fletcher* (1868) and the principle of vicarious liability — arguably unjust because they impose liability without blameworthiness. The circumstances in which a duty of care is owed in negligence can also be explored. One requirement is that it must be fair, just and reasonable to impose a duty. Elements of substantial and formal justice were clearly influential in the decision of *Hill* v *Chief Constable of South Yorkshire* (1991).

Elements of distributive and substantive justice can also be seen in the decision in *Donoghue* v *Stevenson* (1932), in which it was held that a duty of care is owed by the manufacturer to the consumer; and it can be argued that to impose a duty of care on someone who is doing his or her best, as in *Nettleship* v *Weston* (1971) and as required under the principle of *Bolam* (1957), is unjust.

Substantive law: contract

The policy underpinning contract law has increasingly moved away from laissez-faire towards protection of the weaker party. This can be seen through the development of consumer laws by the European Union, national legislation and case law. These laws aim to provide substantive justice and also distributive justice in that rights are given to the weaker party.

There is a wealth of illustrative material that can be used, including the law relating to unfair contract terms and implied terms. Further protection is provided by other legislation including the **Consumer Protection from Unfair Trading Regulations 2008** and the **Cancellation of Contracts made in the Consumer's Home or Place of Work etc. Regulations 2008**.

The role of equity in contracts is relevant to the extent to which justice is achieved. The equitable remedies of specific performance and promissory estoppel were introduced to provide corrective justice where the common law failed to do so.

Conclusion

It is clear that there are aspects of English law where the requirement for formal justice has not been met. This is also true of substantive justice, although arguably less so. However, a balanced view would point out that legislative reform such as the **Human Rights Act 1998** has helped to ensure that procedures are more fair and individuals more likely to experience justice. Arguably, substantive justice does underpin the English legal system, and in the miscarriage of justice cases, for example, it was not the substantive law that was in question but the manner in which it was being administered.

It remains true, of course, that substantive law can be changed through enactment, so that laws regarded as unjust can be repealed. It is not so simple to alter the behaviour of those administering the legal system, making formal justice more difficult to achieve.

> **Knowledge check 15**
>
> What theories of justice are reflected in *Donoghue* v *Stevenson* and protective consumer legislation?

> **Examiner tip**
>
> Questions may ask you to identify obstacles or difficulties with achieving justice. You can discuss these at the end of your essay or refer to them as you discuss individual issues. Obstacles could include inequality of resources, corruption, the withholding of evidence and bias and prejudice as well as the fact that in some situations it is hard to achieve a fair outcome.

Meaning of 'justice':

- dictionary meaning — fairness
- formal (procedural) justice — equality of treatment
- substantive justice — rules must be fair
- distributive justice — fair allocation of benefits and burdens
- corrective justice — righting of wrongs

Theories of justice:

- Aristotle — introduced distributive justice and corrective justice, e.g. miscarriage of justice cases
- natural law theorists (Aquinas) — validity of law depends on conformity with higher law emanating from God, e.g. HRA and right to life conflict in Debbie Purdy case (2009); Professor Lon Fuller — 'inner morality of law' — law must conform to procedural requirements
- utilitarianism (Jeremy Bentham) — greatest happiness of the greatest number — secular, democratic theory, e.g. legislative process; individuals not important.
- positivism (John Austin, Professor Hart) — validity of law not dependent on just or moral content
- John Rawls — just rules made by those placed in original position behind veil of ignorance; promotes liberalism (e.g. HRA) and distributive justice (e.g. government funding); rejects utility
- Marxism and distributive justice — 'From each according to his ability, to each according to his needs'
- Robert Nozick and the minimal state — law should only intervene to protect natural rights

The extent to which justice is achieved:

- Marx, Nozick — not achieved. Other theories — achieved to varying extent.

- Natural justice — each party should be heard, no one should be a judge in his own cause, e.g. judicial independence — Pinochet.
- The rule of law — Dicey — all punishment through courts, no one above the law, e.g. judicial review — *A and Others* (2004).
- Access to justice — cutting funding, e.g. Legal Aid (SPO) Act 2012 prevents formal, substantive, distributive and corrective justice.
- Miscarriages of justice arise from breaches of formal and natural justice, e.g. reluctance to disclose evidence, unreliable forensic evidence (e.g. Sally Clark).
- Criminal justice system — appeal system provides corrective justice, e.g. Birmingham Six, Sally Clark, Sam Hallam — CCRC less effective due to cuts.
- Justice for victims — CJA relaxation of double jeopardy rule aids corrective justice, e.g. Stephen Lawrence. Corrective justice through compensation, e.g. *A v Hoare* (2008).
- Juries — independence promotes natural justice; problems (e.g. jury nobbling) prevent corrective justice. Contempt of Court Act provides corrective justice, e.g. Thoedora Dallas.
- Substantive criminal law: intoxication. Substantially unjust — conviction possible when unable to form *mens rea*.
- Substantive law: tort. Nuisance, *Rylands* v *Fletcher*, vicarious liability substantially unjust — impose liability without fault. Duty of care criteria substantially just.
- Substantive law: contract — distributive justice, e.g. strengthen weaker party in consumer law; corrective justice, e.g. remedies.

Judicial creativity

Characteristics of the doctrine of precedent which limit judicial creativity

Requirement to follow previous decisions

The doctrine of precedent is based on the idea of *stare decisis*, which means to stand by what has been decided. The courts are bound to follow the decisions made in earlier cases. The doctrine of precedent operates within a hierarchical court structure, with the lower courts being bound by the precedents made in the higher courts. The binding part of the judgement is called the *ratio decidendi*, meaning the legal reason for the decision.

Lord Denning campaigned for many years to free the Court of Appeal from being bound by its own decisions and by the House of Lords, in order to allow greater flexibility. The essence of his argument was that once a precedent is set by the House of Lords, only the House of Lords can change it, yet most cases never reach the House of Lords. During his campaign, Lord Denning refused to follow binding decisions of both the Court of Appeal and the House of Lords. While generally agreeing with the principles of his decisions, he was usually rebuked by the Law Lords for disregarding the rules. On one occasion, Lord Cross said: 'It is not for any inferior court — be it a County Court or a division of the Court of Appeal presided over by Lord Denning — to review the decisions of this House. Such a review can only be undertaken by this House itself under the declaration of 1966.'

The requirement of the lower courts to follow precedent was emphasised by the Court of Appeal (Civil Division) in *Barr* v *Biffa* (2012). The High Court had decided in favour of Biffa, partly basing its decision on rules it created in the case. The Court of Appeal reversed the decision and was critical of the creative approach taken by the High Court. Lord Justice Carnwath pointed out that the judge should have confined himself to 'assessing the evidence against the established legal principles' and left the creation of new precedents to the higher courts.

Judges are dependent on cases being brought before the courts

Judges are dependent on cases being brought before them in the higher courts for the opportunity to create law. For example, judges had felt since the 1960s that the old rule of a builder not owing a duty in tort to the person to whom he sold a property was unfair. In *Dutton* v *Bognor Regis UDC* (1972), Lord Denning said *in obiter* that the builder should owe a duty of care, but the opportunity to follow this persuasive precedent did not arise until 1978 in *Batty* v *Metropolitan Property Realisations Ltd*.

Examiner tip

It is important to recognise that this topic is based on the ideas of precedent and statutory interpretation studied as part of AS Unit 1. Your answer will have to move beyond this material but it must have a firm content base derived from it. It is unlikely that you will do well on this topic if you are not familiar with the AS material.

Examiner tip

It is useful to begin your answer by identifying the important features of precedent — hierarchy; *ratio* and *obiter*; binding and persuasive precedent — but then to move quickly into considering which aspects of the rules of precedent limit and which aspects encourage judges to be creative, i.e. to make new rules of law.

Characteristics of the doctrine of precedent which aid judicial creativity

Practice Statement

Under the 1966 Practice Statement, the House of Lords (now the Supreme Court) has the power to depart from its previous decisions when it appears 'right to do so'. The Law Lords have used this power sparingly because of an overall desire to achieve certainty in the law.

However, despite the limitations set out in the Practice Statement and the self-imposed restraint which has characterised the Law Lords in a majority of cases heard since 1966, it has been used to bring about significant changes in the law. Notable examples are that occupiers have some duty in respect of trespassers, *British Railways Board* v *Herrington* (1972); that no participant can use duress as a defence to a murder charge, *R* v *Howe* (1987); that *Hansard* can in certain circumstances be referred to when interpreting a statute, *Pepper* v *Hart* (1993); and that the *mens rea* of recklessness should always be subjective, *R* v *G* (2004).

Overruling

Higher courts can always overrule earlier precedents set in lower courts. Overruling must not be confused with reversing, which involves a higher court changing the outcome of a case on appeal.

Distinguishing

Judges in all courts may avoid following a precedent by finding that the facts of the case before them are materially different from those of the case in which the binding precedent was set. In *Balfour* v *Balfour* (1919), Mrs Balfour was unable to enforce a maintenance agreement made with her husband. The *ratio decidendi* of the case was that there is no intention to create legal relations when agreements are made within marriage. In *Merritt* v *Merritt* (1970), the defendant husband sought to rely on the Balfour principle to avoid honouring an agreement he had made with his estranged wife. The court distinguished the case on the material difference that the agreement, albeit made within marriage, had been made after the couple had separated. The decision limited the scope of the Balfour principle and created a new rule in respect of separated couples.

Dissenting judgements

Judges in the higher courts may disagree with the legal principles being applied in cases before them. In such cases, they may deliver a dissenting judgement, in which they outline principles they believe should apply. Dissenting judgements are persuasive precedents and so may be followed in future cases. Some key areas of law have developed from such judgements. The law on negligent misstatement was developed from the dissenting judgement of Lord Denning in *Candler* v *Crane Christmas* (1951). The majority judges held that accountants, who prepared a company's accounts

Knowledge check 16

What power was given to the House of Lords in the 1966 Practice Statement?

Examiner tip

Other examples of distinguishing could be used instead, e.g. the 'tattooing' case of *Wilson* (distinguished from the sadomasochism case of *Brown*). What is important is that you use some cases to illustrate the points you make.

Knowledge check 17

In which courts can judges be creative through distinguishing?

knowing that they would be relied upon by third parties, owed no duty of care. Lord Denning, however, stipulated the circumstances in which such a duty should be owed. His judgement formed the basis of the decision in *Hedley Byrne* v *Heller* (1964), in which it was held that, had there not been a disclaimer, the claimants could have recovered compensation for economic loss caused by a negligent misstatement. The circumstances outlined in *Caparo* v *Dickman* (1990) for when such a duty should be owed are very similar to those originally outlined by Lord Denning.

Other persuasive precedents

When delivering their judgements, judges sometimes speculate on what their decision would have been had the facts been slightly different. These *obiter* statements are persuasive and may become the *ratio decidendi* of future cases. In *R* v *Brown* (1993) the defendants, who had engaged in sadomasochistic activities, were unable to rely on the defence of consent when prosecuted under the **Offences Against the Person Act 1861**. However, the Lords stated *in obiter* that consent could be a defence to painful practices such as tattooing and piercing. In *R* v *Wilson* (1996), the defendant husband was able to rely on this defence when he used a hot knife to brand his initials onto his wife's buttocks at her request. The Court of Appeal held that the defendant was engaged in body decoration, which was similar to body piercing or tattooing.

Other examples include *R* v *R* (1991), where the House of Lords was influenced by Court of Appeal arguments on the issue of rape within marriage, and *Attorney General for Jersey* v *Holley* (2005), in which the Privy Council was influential in developing the defence of provocation, in spite of conflicting House of Lords authority.

Decisions of superior courts in other jurisdictions can also be persuasive. In *R (Guardian News and Media Limited)* v *City of Westminster Magistrates' Court* (2012) the Court of Appeal held that access should be permitted to documents which had been placed before a court and referred to in open proceedings. In delivering the leading judgement, Toulson LJ referred to the decisions of superior courts in several other common law countries including Canada, New Zealand and South Africa, and explained that these decisions provided 'strong persuasive authority'. He said: 'This case provides a good example of the benefit which can be gained from knowledge of the development of the common law elsewhere'.

The Court of Appeal

In practice, the Court of Appeal makes a great deal of new law because it hears far more cases than the Supreme Court. A good example is *R* v *Woollin* (1998), which clarified the law on oblique intent and has become the leading judgement, despite several earlier House of Lords decisions. It was also the Court of Appeal in *R* v *Prentice* (1994) that effectively reintroduced gross negligence manslaughter into the modern law.

Knowledge check 18

Why does the Court of Appeal have more opportunity to create law than the House of Lords?

Areas of law developed by judges

Evidence of the ability of judges to be creative and develop the law, despite the constraints of precedent, is provided by the fact that in a number of significant areas of law, almost all the rules are judge-made. This presents an opportunity to refer to areas of substantive law in detail. For example, in criminal law, the rules on the *mens rea* of murder, on involuntary manslaughter and on defences such as intoxication and self-defence may be considered. In contract law, examples include the rules on formation and discharge of contracts. In tort, students could refer to areas such as the rules relating to nervous shock or economic loss, private nuisance and the rule in *Rylands* v *Fletcher*. Another area of tort that judges have begun to develop is invasion of privacy. In actions brought under Article 8 of the European Convention on Human Rights — the right to respect for private and family life — a number of celebrities have successfully claimed against newspapers that have published photographs of them in their private life without consent. Cases include *Murray* v *Express Newspapers and Another* (2008) brought by the author J. K. Rowling and her husband, and *Mosley* v *News Group Newspapers Ltd* (2008), in which the Formula One boss successfully sued the *News of the World* in respect of an article headed 'F1 boss has sick Nazi orgy with 5 hookers'.

The extent to which judges display creativity in statutory interpretation

The literal rule

Supporters of the literal rule argue that judges should apply statutes as written in all circumstances. Judges who follow the literal rule are not creative and do not develop the law, even when common sense demands it. An example is *Fisher* v *Bell* (1961). A shopkeeper was charged under the **Offensive Weapons Act 1959** for offering for sale an offensive weapon. He had displayed flick knives in the shop window. The court held that no offence had been committed as, according to contract law, what he had done amounted to an invitation to treat and not to an offer.

The mischief rule

When interpreting a statute, judges may be creative in that they broaden or narrow its application. This is particularly relevant in terms of the mischief and purposive approaches. The mischief rule requires judges to look back to the law before the Act in question was made in order to determine the gap in the law that the Act was intended to remedy. In *Smith* v *Hughes* (1960), a prostitute was prosecuted under the **Street Offences Act 1958** for soliciting in the street. She had attracted the attention of men who were in the street by tapping on her first-floor window. The court held that the mischief the Act had been passed to prevent was men in the street being accosted by prostitutes, and that therefore she was guilty. The Act was thus made broader in application because it was not limited to situations where the prostitute was in the street itself.

A further example is *Royal College of Nursing* v *DHSS* (1981). The **Abortion Act 1967** stated that lawful abortion requires that a pregnancy 'is terminated by a registered medical practitioner'. In 1967, the method of producing an abortion was surgical and so would have needed to be performed by a doctor. However, by the 1980s abortions

Examiner tip
Answers could also refer to the golden rule, which allows more creativity than the literal rule.

were being induced by drip-feeding a drug which caused the fetus to be discharged from the uterus. This was performed by midwives and nurses. The House of Lords held that the mischief the Act had been passed to prevent was illegal, backstreet abortion, and that therefore it was legal for midwives and nurses to administer the drug.

The purposive approach

The purposive approach to legislation has become increasingly popular among English judges, particularly since the UK joined the European Union, because EU law is stated in general principles that can be applied to a broad range of circumstances and it is important, as emphasised by Lord Denning in *Bulmer* v *Bollinger* (1974), that English judges take a purposive approach to interpreting Acts of Parliament which have been passed to comply with European obligations.

The European Convention on Human Rights is similarly set out in broad terms. The judges in the European Court of Human Rights therefore also use the purposive approach. The **Human Rights Act 1998** requires that all legislation be interpreted so that, as far as possible, it is compatible with the convention. This will inevitably result in English judges increasingly using the purposive approach.

In *Yemshaw* v *London Borough of Hounslow* (2011) the purposive approach was used to interpret the meaning of 'violence' in section 177(1) of the **Housing Act 1996**. The Supreme Court said the purpose of the legislation is to ensure that a person is not obliged to remain living in a home where he/she and/or other members of the household are at risk of harm and this purpose would be fulfilled by an updated interpretation of the word 'violence'.

Since the decision in *Pepper* v *Hart* (1993) judges have been able to refer to *Hansard* in limited circumstances, as an aid to interpretation. It would seem this decision was influenced by the shift from the literal to the purposive approach and it has certainly facilitated the latter.

Examiner tip

Other examples of the purposive approach include cases like *Coltman* v *Bibby Tankers, Jones* v *Tower Boot, R* v *Registrar General ex parte Smith* (1990) and *R (Quintavalle)* v *Secretary of State* (2003).

Knowledge check 19

Which approach to statutory interpretation allows for the most judicial creativity?

The balance between the roles of Parliament and the judiciary

The constitutional position

Constitutionally, it is the role of Parliament to create law and, as Lord Radcliffe said, 'it is unacceptable constitutionally that there should be two sources of law-making at work at the same time'. The basis of the constitutional position is that Parliament is democratically elected (at least, the House of Commons is) and that the legislative programme should to some extent be influenced by the electorate. Judges, on the other hand, are not elected.

The constitutional role of judges has changed in recent years through the UK's membership of the European Union. Section 2(4) of the **European Communities Act 1972** states that European Community law should take precedence over English law. In giving effect to this section, English judges have been able to exercise powers

Examiner tip

Exam questions will require you to consider the extent to which judges should be creative. This will involve discussing the role of judges and how this relates to the role of Parliament.

that were not available to them in the past. For example, in *R v Secretary of State for Transport ex parte Factortame* (1990), the European Court of Justice held that domestic courts are entitled to ignore provisions of domestic legislation which are in conflict with provisions of directly enforceable European law. In this case it was also held that domestic courts could suspend domestic legislation while awaiting a decision of the European Court of Justice.

The **Human Rights Act 1998** has also significantly altered the balance between the judges and Parliament. Section 3 requires legislation to be interpreted so that, as far as possible, it is compatible with the European Convention on Human Rights. This was demonstrated in *A and others v Secretary of State for the Home Department* (2004). The House of Lords held that s.23 of the **Anti-Terrorism, Crime and Security Act 2001**, in permitting the detention of suspected international terrorists indefinitely without charge or trial, was incompatible with Articles 5 and 14 of the European Convention on Human Rights.

Sometimes judicial decisions prompt Parliament to legislate. For example, provisions of the **Protection of Freedoms Act 2012** which relate to the keeping of DNA of people not convicted of criminal offences were introduced following the ECHR decision in *S & Marper v UK* (2008) and a declaration by the Supreme Court in 2011 that existing guidelines were unlawful because they were incompatible with the European Convention on Human Rights.

> **Knowledge check 20**
>
> How has the Human Rights Act 1998 increased the law-making role of judges?

Policy

Formulation of policy is the role of Parliament. Policy is a set of ideas about what should be done and sets out objectives and intended directions of change. However, judges are sometimes placed in positions where they have to make policy decisions. First, judges have a role in judicial review and as guardians of individual rights. By giving priority to individual rights over policy, and thereby ruling against the government, they will be making decisions which could be seen as being political and which have an impact on policy goals. For example, the House of Lords' decision in *A and others v Secretary of State for the Home Department* (December 2004) had an impact on how the government deals with terrorism.

> **Knowledge check 21**
>
> Why should the judiciary not formulate policy?

The second problem for judges is that they sometimes have to make controversial decisions, which will inevitably have policy implications. For example, in *Gillick v West Norfolk and Wisbech Area Health Authority* (1986), the issue for the judges to decide was whether or not girls under the age of 16 should be prescribed contraceptives without parental consent.

Policy in statutory interpretation

Judges who favour the literal rule usually justify it on the grounds that they should not change the wording of statutes, because to do so would be to usurp the legislative function and that is not their role. If the outcome of a judicial decision is unsatisfactory, the proper solution is for Parliament to make the legislative change.

On the other hand, there are examples of decisions in statutory interpretation which are based on policy. In *Re Sigsworth* (1935), the Court, using the golden rule, held that a man who murdered his mother, who had died intestate, should not benefit from his crime. It was contrary to public policy to allow such an undesirable outcome.

In the case of *Royal College of Nursing* v *DHSS* (1981), the majority in the House of Lords was influenced by what it considered to be the policy of the **Abortion Act 1967**, namely broadening of the grounds of lawful abortion and ensuring that it was carried out with proper skill. The two dissenting judges, Lords Wilberforce and Edmund-Davies, argued that the Act should not be rewritten because it dealt with 'a controversial subject involving moral or social judgements on which opinions strongly differ'. In other words, this was a policy issue, which should be left to Parliament.

Knowledge check 22

Which rule of interpretation prevents judges formulating policy?

Policy in criminal law

Intoxication

In *DPP* v *Majewski* (1977), policy issues were clearly the basis of the decision. Majewski, after drinking alcohol and taking drugs, attacked people in a public house and then the police officers who tried to arrest him. The House of Lords refused to accept the defence of voluntary intoxication on policy grounds. One of the prime purposes of the criminal law is to protect people from violence and to allow voluntary intoxication as a defence would leave the citizen unprotected. Lord Salmon said: 'If there were to be no penal sanction for any injury unlawfully inflicted under the complete mastery of drink or drugs, voluntarily taken, the social consequences would be appalling.'

Policy in tort

The extension of negligence into ever more diverse areas has also led to policy issues being raised. Decisions are justified by reference to wider social or economic considerations rather than to precedent or to legal principles. This is apparent in the law relating to pure economic loss. In *Spartan Steel and Alloys Ltd* v *Martin & Co. Ltd* (1973), Lord Denning openly based his leading judgement on policy. He said:

> At bottom I think the question of recovering economic loss is one of policy. Whenever the courts draw a line to mark out the bounds of duty, they do it as a matter of policy so as to limit the responsibility of the defendant.

Similar policy issues influenced the development of the law relating to nervous shock in *Alcock* v *Chief Constable of South Yorkshire* (1992).

Should judges create law?

Benefits of judicial law-making

Flexibility

It takes many months for an Act of Parliament to be passed. One of the advantages of the common law system is that the law is able to respond to new situations. Within the limits set by precedent and the rules of statutory interpretation, judges are able to develop the law in ways that reflect changing social and technological circumstances. For example, the law has been adapted to deal with the effect of

Examiner tip

An exam question may ask whether judges should make law. This requires you to consider the benefits and the problems posed by judicial law-making. It is also useful to consider the views of the judges themselves. Stronger students will be able to draw on a wide range of arguments and examples.

life support systems on the exact point of death, *R* v *Malcherek and Steel* (1981); and technical developments in the way abortions are carried out, *Royal College of Nursing* v *DHSS* (1981).

In its report published in March 2012 the Joint Committee on Privacy and Injunctions concluded that the law of privacy was more suitable for judicial than parliamentary development. It states: 'We believe that any statutory definition of privacy would risk becoming outdated quickly, would not allow for flexibility on a case-by-case basis and would lead to even more litigation over its interpretation. For these reasons we do not recommend one'.

In contract law, the postal rule has been adapted to deal with instantaneous forms of communication, *Entores* v *Miles Far East* (1955).

In the law of tort, the House of Lords extended the law on nervous shock to cover situations where the secondary victim came upon the 'immediate aftermath', *McLoughlin* v *O'Brian* (1982).

Insufficient parliamentary time

The government will be intent on pushing through a legislative programme that fulfils its political goals. Consequently, non-controversial, politically insignificant reforms to the law are often left aside for many years. For example, despite the work of the Law Commission, the law on non-fatal offences remains unreformed. Similarly, moral issues are often not included in the legislative programme and the judiciary is consequently left to determine whether development of the law is required. This was clearly the case with husband rape. It had long been regarded by society as unacceptable, but successive parliaments had not found time for statutory change. The long-awaited decision was made in *R* v *R* (1991).

Law made by lawyers/experts

Judges are legal experts and thus better equipped to develop the law than Parliament. Because they are trained to apply existing principles and relate developments to the existing law, the law is more likely to remain consistent and coherent.

Parliamentary sovereignty is not compromised

Judicial law-making does not undermine parliamentary sovereignty because Parliament can overrule judicial decisions. Furthermore, a lot of judicial creativity arises from the process of statutory interpretation. For this reason the Joint Committee on Privacy and Injunctions rejects the criticism that privacy law is 'judge made', pointing out that 'it has evolved from the Human Rights Act 1998'.

Problems with judicial law-making

Constitutional position

The constitutional position is that Parliament creates law and the judges apply it. Formulation of policy is the role of a democratically elected parliament which will recognise the will of the electorate. Judges are unelected. In addition, they are arguably not representative of the population. Judges are drawn from a narrow social group and this raises the possibility, identified by Professor Griffith, that they will inevitably have views which reflect this narrow social background. Women and people from ethnic minorities are under-represented, especially among the senior judiciary. For example, there are no Law Lords from ethnic minorities and the only female Law Lord, Lady Hale, was not appointed until 2004.

Lack of research

When Parliament wants to introduce a new piece of legislation, there is considerable opportunity for comprehensive research. Very often, legislation will be the result of recommendations from the Law Reform bodies, which possess the expertise to research an area thoroughly. The Law Commission is a permanent law reform body and has had considerable success in having recommendations recognised in Acts of Parliament. Examples of such legislation include the **Contracts (Rights of Third Parties) Act 1999** and the **Computer Misuse Act 1990**. The Green Paper stage allows for interested parties to be consulted and the passage of the bill through Parliament will involve many debates among people who are able to research the relevant issues. Judges' decisions, however, will be based on the evidence presented to them by the parties involved in the case. They cannot consider arguments about the general social, economic or moral aspects, even though their decision, as in *Gillick* v *West Norfolk and Wisbech Area Health Authority* (1986) for example, may inevitably have implications for society generally.

Judge-made law operates retrospectively

Judge-made law applies to events that have taken place prior to its creation.

In *R* v *R* (1991) an act, which was lawful at the time it was committed, was turned into a serious criminal offence. In *SW and CR* v *United Kingdom* (1995), the ECtHR upheld the decision, saying the UK had not been in breach of Article 7 of the Convention, which states that no one should be found guilty of an offence which was not an offence at the time it was committed. The Court's reasoning was that judicial law-making was well entrenched in legal tradition and the development of the law in this case had been reasonably foreseeable.

The reasoning of the ECtHR was followed by the Court of Appeal in *R* v *Crooks* (2004). The defendant had forced his wife to have sexual intercourse without her consent in 1970, 32 years before his conviction and 21 years before the *R* v *R* decision. Upholding the rape conviction, Judge LJ said that the defendant should have foreseen that the marital exemption was about to be removed. The right of the wife to freedom from inhuman or degrading treatment outweighed the defendant's right not to be tried retrospectively.

This problem does not arise with legislation, which operates prospectively. Legislation usually comes into effect on a fixed date after the Act has received the royal assent, in order to allow time for people to prepare for the law change.

In some countries, including the USA, cases only apply prospectively. In a speech in 1987, the then Lord Chancellor, Lord Mackay, discussed the possibility of allowing

Knowledge check 23

Why is retrospective law-making undesirable?

prospective overruling, whereby the court might uphold the existing precedent in the instant case but declare it overruled for the future. The main problem with this idea is that most litigants would find it hard to accept that they had won their case only for future litigants, not for themselves. There would seem little point in going to court at all.

Judge-made law is incremental in nature

Judges can only make law on the facts of the case before them. They cannot lay down a comprehensive code to cover all similar situations. Some areas of law, for example negligence, might be well suited to this case-by-case approach. However, with other areas it is not helpful when one small change is made, such as the introduction of gross negligence manslaughter in *R* v *Prentice* (1994) and *R* v *Adomako* (1995), when really the whole area of involuntary manslaughter needs to be properly reformed.

Judge-made law thus develops in an unstructured, random way. It is dependent on cases being brought and then appealed through to a court sufficiently senior to make a new precedent.

Complexity/technical distinctions

One of the arguments often used against precedent as a law-making process is that judges make technical distinctions between the case they are deciding and the precedent, in order to avoid following the precedent. The result of this is that the law becomes complex and confusing, with many minor technical distinctions.

Judicial preference

Judicial views on the constitutional position

There are contrasting views among judges on the extent to which they should be making new rules of law. Lord Justice Oliver argued that for judges to develop new concepts of law would be an abandonment by the court of its proper function and an assumption by it of the mantle of legislator. Adopting this view, the courts have resisted pressure to reform the law of assisted suicide. In the Tony Nicklinson case Lord Justice Toulson said, 'To do as Tony wants, the court would be making a major change in the law. It is not for the court to decide whether the law about assisted dying should be changed and, if so, what safeguards should be put in place. Under our system of government these are matters for parliament to decide.' Cases in which the House of Lords has refused to develop the criminal law include *R* v *Jones and Others* (2006) and *R* v *Davis* (2008).

Lord Scarman, by contrast, put forward the view in *McLoughlin* v *O'Brian* (1982) that the court's proper function was to adjudicate according to principle. If principle led to results which were felt to be socially unacceptable, then Parliament could legislate to overrule them. The real risk to the common law would be if it stood still, halted by a conservative judicial approach.

Examiner tip
Individual judges have sometimes commented on the law-making role that judges should have. Brief references to judicial views will enhance the quality of an answer, but you should also cover the wider arguments about the benefits and problems of judicial law-making.

Judicial law-making is more acceptable in some areas of law than others

Some judges argue that the role of the judiciary should be determined by the type of law involved. The view of Lord Reid in the 1960s was that judges should not so readily create new law in areas such as property, contract, family and criminal law, where certainty is of vital importance, but that they could have more freedom to do so in the areas of tort and public and administrative law, where the judges regard their creative role as legitimate and appropriate.

Lord Devlin argued that judges should stick to activist law-making, by which he meant developing the law in line with the consensus view of society, and avoid dynamic law-making, which involved taking sides on controversial issues.

However, judges cannot avoid making decisions in controversial cases. These might be cases which are politically sensitive, such as *Bromley LBC* v *GLC* (1983) and *ex parte Pinochet* (2000), or ones which raise profound moral or social issues, for example *Gillick* v *West Norfolk and Wisbech Area Health Authority* (1986) and *Airedale NHS Trust* v *Bland* (1993). In practice, judges have to get involved in controversial areas because such cases are brought before the courts. It is difficult to see how, in deciding any of these cases, judges could have avoided engaging in dynamic law-making and offending at least one section of the community.

Personal preference

Judges adopt contrasting views on their role and it is difficult to escape the conclusion that the view they take is largely a matter of personal preference. Lord Denning, in particular, had a crusading approach to judicial law-making and he was determined not to be fettered by existing legal rules. He argued that it was the duty of judges to do justice and not to follow unjust precedents or restrictive approaches to statutory interpretation. But he was firmly opposed by senior Law Lords, including Viscount Simmonds, who described his approach to statutory interpretation of 'filling in the gaps' as a 'naked usurpation of the legislative function'. David Robertson, writing in 1998, concluded: 'Law in almost any case that comes before the Lords turns out to be whatever their Lordships feel it ought to be.'

Conclusion

It is evident that, in some respects, Parliament is more suited than the judiciary to develop the law. However, areas of the law which are largely judge-made seem to work just as well as those made almost exclusively by Parliament. Through the doctrine of precedent and their role in statutory interpretation, judges frequently have to develop the law by clarifying, and in some cases putting right, what is written in an Act of Parliament.

Examiner tip
Your conclusion will depend on the specific aspects that the question asks you to consider and it should reflect the broad arguments that you have used in the body of the essay.

Summary

Characteristics of the doctrine of precedent which limit judicial creativity:

- requirement to follow previous decisions — *stare decisis*; court hierarchy
- judges dependent on cases being brought before the courts, e.g. *Batty* v *Metropolitan Property Realisations Ltd*

Characteristics of the doctrine of precedent which aid judicial creativity:

- Practice Statement 1966, e.g. *R* v *Howe*
- overruling
- distinguishing, e.g. *Balfour* v *Balfour* and *Merritt* v *Merritt*
- dissenting judgements — negligent misstatement developed from dissenting judgement in *Candler* v *Crane Christmas*
- other persuasive precedents: *obiter dicta*, e.g. *R* v *Brown* and *R* v *Wilson*; decisions of lower courts, e.g. *R* v *R* (1991); decisions of superior courts in other jurisdictions, e.g. *Guardian* newspaper case (2012)
- the Court of Appeal — a creative court, e.g. *R* v *Woollin* oblique intent

The extent to which judges display creativity in statutory interpretation:

- literal rule — not creative, e.g. *Fisher* v *Bell*
- mischief rule — creative, e.g. *Smith* v *Hughes*
- purposive approach — follows European approach — creative, e.g. *Yemshaw* (2011)

The balance between the roles of Parliament and the judiciary:

- the constitutional position — role of judges to apply law made by Parliament
- but effect of European Union and the Human Rights Act, e.g. *Factortame* case, *Marper* v *UK*

Policy:

- formulation of policy is role of Parliament, but judicial review, e.g. *A and others* v *SS for the Home Department*

- policy in statutory interpretation: no policy decisions using literal rule; policy decisions using golden rule, e.g. *Sigsworth*; mischief rule, e.g. *Royal College of Nursing* case; purposive approach
- policy in criminal law — intoxication, e.g. *Majewski*
- policy in tort — economic loss, e.g. *Spartan Steel*

Should judges create law?

- Benefits of judicial law-making:
  - flexibility, e.g. life support systems (e.g. *R* v *Malcherek and Steel*)
  - insufficient parliamentary time, e.g. non-fatal offences
  - law made by lawyers/experts
  - parliamentary sovereignty not compromised — Parliament can overrule judicial decisions
- Problems with judicial law-making:
  - constitutional position — judicial role to apply law made by Parliament
  - lack of research — limited to evidence presented during the case
  - judge-made law retrospective — unfair, e.g. *R* v *R*, *R* v *Crooks* (2004)
  - judge-made law incremental in nature — small changes not helpful, e.g. gross negligence manslaughter (e.g. *R* v *Adomako*)
  - complexity/technical distinctions — make law confusing

Judicial preference:

- differing judicial views on the constitutional position
- judicial law-making more acceptable in some areas of law than others, e.g. generally not acceptable in crime
- personal preference — some judges more creative, e.g. Lord Denning, others less so

Fault

The meaning of 'fault'

There are various definitions of 'fault'. The *Concise Oxford Dictionary* provides many: 'defect, imperfection, blemish, of character...thing wrongly done...responsibility for something wrong...blame'. The *Collins Concise Dictionary* provides similar definitions: 'responsibility for a mistake or misdeed...guilty of error, culpable...blame'.

While there are various definitions of fault, perhaps the core meaning is 'responsibility'. The definition, 'responsibility for something wrong', would appear to be the most useful for the purposes of discussing the role of fault in English law.

Fault in criminal law

There are some aspects of criminal law that seem to show that fault is very important, but there are other aspects that indicate confusion or lack of consistency in the application of fault and there are aspects where the fault element seems to be absent.

Evidence that fault is important in criminal law

Actus reus

To be found guilty of most criminal offences, an *actus reus* must be present and it could be argued that a person who does not actually carry out their criminal intent is not at fault. Also, in order to be found guilty of a criminal offence, the accused must commit the *actus reus* voluntarily. If the accused is not in control of his or her own actions, then he or she cannot be said to be acting voluntarily or at fault. There are criminal defences, including automatism (e.g. *R* v *Bailey*, 1983) and duress (e.g. *R* v *Hudson & Taylor*, 1971), which the accused may plead in such circumstances, proof of which will result in acquittal. The accused will thus not be held responsible for actions which are not the result of his or her rational will.

The rules of causation are linked to fault because they are based on the responsibility of the defendant for the consequences. The defendant is not responsible for the consequence if there is an intervening act which breaks the chain of causation. In circumstances where an intervening act of the victim breaks the chain of causation the victim is seen as responsible for the consequences because he/she does an act 'so daft as to make it his own voluntary act' — Stuart Smith LJ in *R* v *Williams & Davis* (1992).

The rules on omissions are also linked to fault. The general rule is that there is no liability for a failure to act. But in some circumstances it could be argued that the person who does nothing is at fault and this is reflected in the exceptions to the general rule: for example, where there is a duty to act under a contract (e.g. *R* v *Pittwood*, 1902) or where a duty to act has arisen in respect of a voluntary assumption of care (e.g. *Stone & Dobinson*, 1977).

> **Examiner tip**
> Fault questions need to be answered with reference to examples selected from any areas of law. Questions will never specify criminal or civil law and you are free to select the areas that you feel illustrate the principles best. In these notes we consider the role of fault in criminal law and then in the law of tort, but other areas could be used, e.g. contract law.

> **Examiner tip**
> Exam questions are likely to ask you to consider the extent to which fault is needed or is important. You therefore need to relate your discussion of criminal law rules to the idea of fault.

> **Knowledge check 24**
> What aspects of *actus reus* demonstrate the importance of fault in criminal law?

Mens rea

Mens rea is the aspect of criminal law that most obviously illustrates the need for fault to be proved. The *mens rea* is the mental element of the criminal offence and is usually defined in terms of intention or recklessness. The state of mind required for a conviction varies from one offence to another, but the criminal law recognises that a person who acts without the necessary mental awareness is not at fault. For example, in *R* v *Clarke* (1972) the defendant successfully claimed a lack of *mens rea* as a result of absent-mindedness arising from depression.

Intention can be either direct, where the purpose of the accused is to bring about the prohibited consequence, or indirect (oblique), where the accused recognises the result is a virtual certainty and yet continues with the act. This principle was set out in *R* v *Nedrick* and confirmed in *R* v *Woollin*.

Recklessness can be defined as unjustified risk-taking and is now always considered as subjective following the House of Lords judgement in *R* v *G* (2004), which abolished Caldwell recklessness. Subjective recklessness requires the defendant knowingly to take a risk.

Examiner tip

When discussing *mens rea* it is important to explain that there are different levels of *mens rea* and that therefore there is not one consistently applied idea of fault.

Murder and voluntary manslaughter

Murder is the most serious homicide offence. The accused must have had the intention to kill or to cause grievous bodily harm. The law recognises that the person who intends to kill or cause serious injury is more at fault than for example a person who kills recklessly or carelessly and this is reflected in the mandatory sentence of life imprisonment.

Partial defences specific to murder allow a conviction for voluntary manslaughter. The partial defences of diminished responsibility (**Homicide Act 1957** s.2 as amended by s.52 of the **Coroners and Justice Act 2009**) and loss of control (**Coroners and Justice Act 2009** s.54) apply to situations where the accused is considered not to be totally in control of what he or she is doing. A person who kills deliberately as a result of an abnormality of mental functioning is considered less at fault, as is a person who kills deliberately as a result of having a justifiable sense of being seriously wronged or because of fear of serious violence. The less serious nature of voluntary manslaughter is recognised through the life sentence being discretionary rather than mandatory.

Knowledge check 25

Why does proof of the partial defences to murder result in a conviction for manslaughter?

Defences

Further evidence of the importance of fault in criminal liability is the existence of general defences. Some defences, such as self-defence, result in complete acquittal and reflect the fact that a person who is acting to protect him/herself or others or is seeking to prevent a crime and only uses reasonable force should not be considered to be at fault at all. As clarified in *R* v *Williams* (Gladstone, 1987) a defendant who acts even under an honest mistaken view of the facts is not criminally responsible for those acts even if the mistake is objectively unreasonable. The defendant's actions are not regarded as his or her fault.

Voluntary intoxication may act as a partial defence to crimes of specific intent as long as the defendant is unable to form the *mens rea* (e.g. *DPP* v *Majewski*, 1977). The effect of the intoxication renders the defendant less responsible for his or her actions, but he or she will still be guilty of the basic level offence (e.g. Section 20 **Offences Against the Person Act 1861** instead of Section 18). A person who becomes intoxicated involuntarily to the extent that he or she cannot form the *mens rea* is considered to be even less at fault (e.g. *R* v *Kingston*, 1994) and would have a complete defence to any crime.

Areas of law where the fault element is inconsistent or less clear

Involuntary manslaughter

Involuntary manslaughter is much more difficult to classify in terms of fault. To be convicted of unlawful and dangerous act manslaughter the defendant need only have the *mens rea* for the unlawful act which may be as little as battery — Mitchell. Furthermore, now that the definition of recklessness is subjective, following *R* v *G* (2004), it is hard to see how the objective test in the definition of 'dangerous' in this offence can be justified. The definition of 'dangerous' is that given in *R* v *Church* (1967) as meaning 'in the sense that a sober and reasonable person would inevitably recognise that it carried some risk of harm'. So a person could be guilty if a sober and reasonable person thought his or her actions were dangerous, even if the person him/herself did not appreciate the danger.

The *mens rea* for gross negligence manslaughter is gross negligence, which is not fully defined. Lord Mackay in *R* v *Adomako* (1995) was unwilling to provide a detailed definition of gross negligence. However, he quoted Lord Hewart CJ, who in *R* v *Bateman* (1925) stated that it was 'such disregard for the life and safety of others as to amount to a crime against the State and conduct deserving punishment'. In *R* v *Singh* (1999) it is clear that the test can be an objective one — whether a reasonably prudent person would have foreseen a serious and obvious risk of death.

Both types of involuntary manslaughter therefore have significant objective elements, and thus seem to be out of step with most other important areas of criminal law. The rules have been criticised by the Law Commission as unsatisfactory.

Non-fatal offences

The operation of fault in non-fatal offences is also inconsistent. It is clear that all of the offences require proof of fault for a conviction. However, while some of the offences have a *mens rea* requirement which equates with the harm caused, others do not.

Assault and battery require intention or subjective recklessness to bring about the prohibited result of the *actus reus*. However, sections 47 and 20 of the **Offences Against the Person Act 1861** both require intention or recklessness to bring about a result less serious than that specified in the *actus reus*. If charged with a s.47 offence, the accused can be found guilty of causing actual bodily harm, despite having only the intention or subjective recklessness to cause an assault or battery. Under s.20, a

Examiner tip
Mark schemes are likely to have two potential contents, the first wanting (in simple terms) evidence that fault is required and the second wanting evidence that sometimes it is not required. These comments about involuntary manslaughter and non-fatal offences would probably be credited in the second potential content because they seem to question the role of fault.

Knowledge check 26

In what way are sections 47 and 20 of the Offences Against the Person Act 1861 and constructive manslaughter similar in terms of the fault requirement?

conviction can be sustained for wounding or causing grievous bodily harm when the accused only intended or took the risk of causing some harm. Under sections 47 and 20, the accused is thus held legally responsible for a level of harm higher than that he or she is at fault in bringing about.

Aspects of criminal law which seem to go against the fault principle

The distinction between legal fault and motive

In criminal law, the legal fault requirement is stipulated in the definition of the offences. However, criminal law takes no account of motive. This is illustrated clearly by the issue of mercy killings. People who perpetrate mercy killings do so out of care for the victim and often with the best possible motive, but they will still be technically guilty of murder because they have killed deliberately.

In *R v Cox* (1992), Dr Cox was found guilty of attempted murder. He had injected a terminally ill, elderly patient who was suffering constant severe pain, with a lethal drug, after the patient asked him to end her suffering. Where possible, the judge may take account of motive when sentencing, and Dr Cox was given a suspended prison sentence.

The thin skull rule

Application of the 'eggshell skull' rule results in the defendant's liability going beyond that indicated by his or her level of fault. The defendant is criminally responsible for consequences which are far more serious than those which could have been foreseen and the fault of the victim is irrelevant. In *R v Blaue* (1975) the defendant stabbed the victim who then refused a life-saving blood transfusion due to religious beliefs. In such cases the fault of the victim is not relevant. The defendant's conviction for manslaughter was upheld on appeal.

Strict liability offences

There are many crimes for which there is no fault requirement in terms of *mens rea*. This is a significant departure from the principle that to be guilty of a criminal offence a defendant should be proved to be at fault.

Strict liability offences are generally regulatory offences, concerned with public safety, and usually made by statute. They cover situations such as minor road traffic offences, food safety laws, protection of the environment, and the sale of alcohol and tobacco to underage children.

In *Harrow LBC v Shah* (1999), the defendant, a newsagent, was convicted of selling a lottery ticket to a 13-year-old. The fact that he had told staff not to sell lottery tickets to under-16s, had put up a notice in the shop to this effect, and had told staff to ask for proof of identity was irrelevant.

While legislation may impose strict liability for crimes which are truly criminal in nature, in the absence of such provision the courts are reluctant to do so.

In such situations there is a presumption that *mens rea* is required. This principle is illustrated in cases such as *B* v *DPP* (2000).

While strict liability offences do not require *mens rea* they do require an *actus reus*. The *actus reus* must be committed voluntarily so it would appear that even strict liability offences are dependent on proof of fault, albeit to a lesser extent.

Absolute liability offences

Absolute liability offences, sometimes referred to as 'state of affairs' offences, do not require *mens rea* and do not require the act to be carried out voluntarily. In *Winzar* v *Chief Constable of Kent* (1983), the accused was charged with being found drunk on the highway. He had entered a hospital while drunk and had been asked to leave. When he refused, the police were called. The police forcefully removed him from the hospital to their car, which was parked on the highway. He was convicted, despite having been forced by the police to commit the offence.

Mandatory sentences

Mandatory sentences for murder under the **Crime (Sentencing) Act 1997** would also appear to go against the principle that decisions in criminal law should be based on the amount of fault displayed by the defendant. The mandatory life sentence for murder has been widely criticised, particularly in the context of 'mercy killing' cases such as *R* v *Cox* (1992), and in 1989 a House of Lords select committee recommended its abolition. The 1997 Act has been challenged under the **Human Rights Act 1998**. It imposes automatic sentences for subsequent offences. These automatic sentences can only be avoided in 'exceptional' circumstances. In *R* v *Offen* (2001), in order to prevent a possible breach of Article 3 or 5, the Court of Appeal interpreted 'exceptional' to mean any case where there was not a danger to the public, thus significantly weakening the scope of the Act to impose automatic sentences for subsequent offences.

Despite the criticism of mandatory sentences, they have been retained by subsequent legislation. For example, s.225 of the **Criminal Justice Act 2003** imposes an automatic life sentence if a person is convicted of a second serious violent or sexual offence.

Fault in the law of tort

Aspects of tort that illustrate the importance of fault

Negligence

For a claimant to succeed in an action of negligence, three elements must be proved: duty of care, breach and causation. In deciding whether there has been a breach of duty, the courts consider whether the 'reasonable man' would have behaved as the defendant did. A defendant not behaving as the 'reasonable man' would be seen to have been at fault.

Knowledge check 27
What is the defining aspect of strict liability offences?

Knowledge check 28
In what way do mandatory sentences go against the fault principle?

Examiner tip
A whole answer could be written just referring to tort. Alternatively, you could base the bulk of your answer on tort, but also make reference to criminal or contract law.

Knowledge check 29

Why were the defendants in *Bolton* v *Stone* not at fault?

In *Bolton* v *Stone* (1951), the claimant had been hit by a cricket ball. The court considered the likelihood of the risk of injury to be very small on the basis that balls had flown out of the cricket ground between six and ten times in 30 years. The court decided that the 'reasonable man' would have acted the same way and would not have taken further preventative measures.

Occupiers' liability

Occupiers' liability is also based on reasonableness. An occupier fulfils the duty owed to visitors and non-visitors under the **Occupiers' Liability Acts 1957** and **1984** by taking reasonable precautions. In *Martin* v *Middlesbrough Corporation* (1965), the council was held liable to the child claimant who slipped in a playground and cut herself on a broken glass bottle. The council did not have adequate arrangements in place for the disposal of such litter.

Under s.2(2)(b), people on the premises in the exercise of their calling are owed a lower duty of care, since they are expected to know what they are doing. There is a shift in responsibility from the occupier to the visitor. In *Roles* v *Nathan* (1963), chimney sweeps had been hired to clean central heating flues. They were warned of danger from fumes but entered the chimney and died. The occupiers were not liable since they were not at fault. The sweeps were acting in the exercise of their calling, so it was their responsibility to know about the dangers.

An occupier is considered to be less at fault if a trespasser is injured than if the victim is a lawful visitor. This is reflected in the **Occupiers' Liability Act 1984**, which limits the duty owed to trespassers to the following circumstances:
- the occupier is aware that a danger exists
- the occupier is aware that the trespasser is in the vicinity of the danger
- the danger is of a kind that the occupier should guard against in all circumstances

Knowledge check 30

Why were the defendants in *Martin* v *Middlesbrough Corporation* at fault?

While the courts are more sympathetic to child trespassers, the courts' reluctance to impose liability in respect of trespassers is evident from cases such as *Tomlinson* v *Congleton BC* (2003). The unsuccessful claimant, aged 18, dived into a lake in a public park and suffered a severe spinal injury. The council had placed warning signs and was planning to make the lake inaccessible to the public when the accident occurred.

Fault of the victim: contributory negligence and *volenti non fit injuria*

In apportioning damages in tort, the law takes into account the fault of the victim. Section 1(1) of the **Law Reform (Contributory Negligence) Act 1945** states that where any person suffers damage as the result partly of his own fault, the damages recoverable shall be reduced to such an extent as the court thinks just and equitable, having regard to the claimant's share in the responsibility for the damage.

In *Froom* v *Butcher* (1976), the claimant's damages were reduced by 25%. He had been involved in a vehicle accident caused by the negligence of the defendant, but was partly responsible for his injuries, as he had not been wearing a seat belt.

The essential elements of *volenti* are that the victim knows of the risk of injury, voluntarily decides to take that risk and expressly or impliedly agrees to waive any claim in respect of such injury. The claimant must be in the position to choose freely. In *Imperial Chemical Industries Ltd v Shatwell* (1965) the claimant and his brother tested a circuit of detonators, ignoring the employer's safety procedures and warnings. There was no interference with the claimant's freedom of choice and his injuries were therefore his fault. The defence does not apply in rescue cases (e.g. *Baker v Hopkins*, 1959) or some employment cases as the claimant cannot be said to have voluntarily accepted the risk. In *Smith v Baker* (1891) the defence of *volenti* was unsuccessful because the employee did not freely and voluntarily consent to the risk posed by a crane moving boulders above his head.

Knowledge check 31

Why does *volenti* not apply in rescue cases and some employment cases?

Aspects of tort that do not require fault

While it can be seen that liability in negligence or occupiers' liability depends upon proof of fault, in other areas of the law of tort this is not the case.

Nuisance

Nuisance is not concerned with the fault of the defendant. Whether the defendant took reasonable care to avoid the nuisance or not is irrelevant. Reasonableness in nuisance is concerned with the level of interference with the claimant's enjoyment of his or her land. However, motive or malice of the defendant is an issue. This is illustrated by *Christie v Davey* (1893). Whenever the claimant gave music lessons, the defendant deliberately shrieked and banged on the adjoining wall. The claimant succeeded because the defendant had acted maliciously.

Rylands v Fletcher (1868)

The rule in *Rylands v Fletcher* originally involved strict liability for damage caused by something escaping from the defendant's land. This rule only applied to non-natural or artificial use of land. In this case, the defendants were liable for escape of water into a mine, even though there was no wrongful intent or negligence. The water constituted a non-natural use, due to the non-natural quantity. However, the case of *Cambridge Water Co. Ltd v Eastern Counties Leather* (1994) introduced a fault requirement. The House of Lords held that defendants would only be liable for damage of a foreseeable type.

Knowledge check 32

What fault requirement was introduced into the rule in *Rylands v Fletcher* by the *Cambridge Water Co.* case?

Vicarious liability

The principle of vicarious liability imposes liability for someone else's fault. Under this principle, employers can be held vicariously liable for torts committed by their employees in the course of their employment. No liability will be incurred for acts done which are considered to be outside the course of employment or when the employee is considered to be 'on a frolic of his own'. The principle applies in respect of prohibited acts, and acts which are carried out in a prohibited or unauthorised manner. In *Rose v Plenty* (1976), the claimant, aged 13, was helping the defendant deliver milk. This was expressly forbidden by his employers. The claimant was injured through the defendant's employee's negligent driving. The employers were held liable. The employee was doing what he was employed to do, i.e. deliver milk, but he was doing it in an unauthorised manner. While it may appear unfair on the employer,

Examiner tip

Relatively few students venture far beyond negligence when considering the civil law. Stronger students are able to use a wider range of torts, including occupiers' liability, nuisance, *Rylands* v *Fletcher* and the principle of vicarious liability.

who is not at fault, the principle of vicarious liability is justified on the basis that the act is done for the employer's benefit, and the victim is more likely to be compensated due to the requirement of compulsory insurance.

Liability for defective products

Liability for defective products was dependent upon proof of fault until the **Consumer Protection Act 1987** was introduced. Claimants had to prove that the manufacturer was in breach of his or her duty of care. The 1987 Act imposed what is, in effect, strict liability on producers for damage caused by defective product. The producers may therefore be liable even if they have taken all reasonable care.

Moves towards a no-fault-based system for accident victims

In more recent years, there has been a move from the laissez-faire ideal which dominated in the nineteenth century. The law has increasingly come to focus on the injured victim rather than the blameworthy individual. Twentieth-century legislation provides a partial no-fault-based system.

The Welfare State legislation created the Department of Social Security. Victims of accidents at work are now able to claim compensation from the state, without the need to prove negligence. Social security benefits are also available to those who suffer illness or disability.

Should liability in criminal law depend on proof of fault?

Arguments in favour of the requirement of fault in criminal law

The effect of criminal sanctions and procedures

Criminal law is enforced through state procedures and sanctions, focused on the defendant. A guilty verdict will result in the imposition of a sentence on the defendant. The court has a wide range of sentences at its disposal, some of which will directly limit the liberty of the convict, such as electronic tagging, probation and incarceration.

Punishment, however, is only justified if people are at fault. Depriving people of their liberty or imposing other punishments are serious infringements of personal freedom. Furthermore, the liberty of the convicted individual will also be affected by his or her criminal record, which may, for example, prevent access to certain jobs and thus adversely affect opportunities. Opportunities in turn will be affected by the public condemnation of the individual's offence(s). Minor road traffic offences, which are strict liability, do not result in a criminal record, but there is still a stigma attached to strict liability offences, e.g. the butcher who unknowingly sells bad meat.

It is because of these issues that the legal profession, the judges and the legislature regard the principle of no liability without proof of fault as being so important in criminal law.

Strict liability is ineffective

Despite proof of fault being regarded as so important in criminal law, there are some strict liability offences. However, those who argue against strict liability suggest that there is no real evidence that it increases levels of care. This may be partly attributable to the lack of incentive to act reasonably if no account is taken of attempts to prevent the prohibited act occurring. People are also more likely to accept their guilt and punishment if fault has to be proved. In Australia, a defence of all due care is available. Were this defence available in England, it would deal with situations where defendants, such as Mr Shah (in *Harrow LBC v Shah*), take all reasonable care to avoid committing the offence.

Furthermore, the argument that in strict liability offences the penalty is small is dubious. It is inconsistent with justice to convict someone who is not guilty in the normal sense of the word just because the penalty is small.

Strict liability offences can lead to unjust outcomes

Under the **Firearms Act 1968** as amended there is a minimum sentence of 5 years for possession of some prohibited weapons. Possession of some prohibited weapons is a strict liability offence. The legislature is clearly attempting to protect society from a perceived growing threat from gun crime. But the public, the media and the judges can seem to agree that in some circumstances a criminal conviction and sentence is not appropriate. In December 2009 an ex soldier who had handed in a sawn off shotgun he had found dumped in his garden to Reigate police station was given a 12-month suspended sentence.

We could also argue that in cases like *Harrow v Shah* the defendants had done all they could to avoid committing the offence and it is unfair that they were convicted.

The need to restrain the power of the state

An important argument in favour of the fault requirement is that decisions on guilt rest with juries or independent magistrates, and anything that reduces their capacity to make decisions inevitably means that more power rests with the prosecutors. With most strict liability offences, conviction is a formality.

Arguments in favour of the no-fault principle

Protection of the public

Strict liability legislation is usually justified on the basis that it protects the public good, and typically deals with issues such as public health and safety, protection of the environment and road traffic. Another argument is that higher standards of care are encouraged. Social scientist Barbara Wootten has defended strict liability, suggesting that if the objective of the criminal law is to prevent socially damaging activities, it would be absurd to turn a blind eye to those who cause harm because of

Examiner tip
You may be required to consider whether liability should depend on proof of fault. It is important to consider why liability should depend on proof of fault, and the problems that the principle of no liability without proof of fault present.

carelessness or negligence or even by accident. Section 7 of the **Bribery Act 2010** provides that it is an offence for a commercial organisation to fail to prevent bribery. The creation of the offence is justified on the basis it will help to reduce corruption.

Sections 5 to 8 of the **Sexual Offences Act 2003** impose strict liability in respect of sexual offences with children under 13. These offences are of strict liability as to age. The prosecution has only to prove the intentional sexual activity and the age of the victim. As Lord Falconer said during the passage of the Sexual Offences bill, 'the fundamental justification for the under-13 offence is the age and vulnerability of the victim'. In *R* v *G* (not to be confused with the *R* v *G* which concerned reckless manslaughter) the defendant was aged 15 at the time and the victim was aged 12. The defendant honestly believed the victim to be 15. Both the defendant and the victim agreed that the victim had told the defendant she was 15. He was found guilty under section 5 and initially given 12 months' detention, though this was reduced on appeal to a conditional discharge.

Knowledge check 33

Why could the defendant in *R* v *G* be said not to be at fault?

There is also the fact that most strict liability offences carry relatively low sentences in recognition of the lower levels of fault.

Saving of time and expense

There is a further advantage in that court time is saved and consequently costs are reduced when there is no need to prove *mens rea*. Defendants are also more likely to plead guilty. In *Gammon (Hong Kong) Ltd* v *Attorney General of Hong Kong* (1985), the Privy Council said that if the prosecution had to prove *mens rea* in even the smallest regulatory offence, the administration of justice might quickly come to a complete standstill.

Should liability in civil law depend on proof of fault?

In civil law, compensation is regarded as the responsibility of those at fault

Civil law, like criminal law, is based on the notion of individual responsibility. Individuals choose to behave the way they do and should therefore accept responsibility for the outcomes of their actions. Individuals can choose to be more careful so as to minimise the harm they cause. It is unfair to punish an individual for harm caused by an accident, because being more careful would not have prevented the harm and it was not possible for the blameless individual to be more careful. In November 2011 a report to the Department of Work and Pensions highlighted the problem of cases where employees have been awarded compensation despite employers doing everything that is reasonably practicable and foreseeable. The government has conceded that the rules were not fair and announced that it will introduce legislation as a result of the recommendations made in the report.

Gradual move towards a no-fault-based system for accident victims

The advantage of the no-fault-based system for accident victims is that those who are entitled to compensation or social security are more likely to receive it than they would be under the fault-based tort system. It may be fairer for more people to receive compensation, albeit lesser in amount. However, there is the perception of unfairness in that all of society has to pay for what often amounts to the acts of blameworthy individuals.

The Consumer Protection Act 1987

The **Consumer Protection Act 1987** imposes strict liability on producers for damage caused by defective products. This favours the victims, who can recover compensation without the need to prove fault. However, while it is the producer who directly provides the compensation to the claimant, the burden is indirectly borne by society, because as the risk of liability increases, so too will insurance premiums, and this cost will be passed on to consumers.

Insurance premiums

While some victims are able to claim compensation without the need to prove fault, there are many who are still required to do so. Road accident victims and victims of medical errors have to satisfy the negligence requirements, despite the defendants being insured. The insurance issue arguably prevents the extension of no-fault liability as insurance premiums would inevitably have to rise and might become unaffordable. More people would risk driving without insurance and medical practitioners would be less willing to provide anything other than treatment that they considered totally safe.

Conclusion

It would seem that the imposition of liability without fault is more acceptable in civil law than in criminal law. The unfairness of leaving an injured victim without compensation increasingly outweighs the unfairness of blameless individuals being required to provide that compensation indirectly through state funds or insurance.

Despite the arguments against the imposition of strict liability in tort, including the doubt that it raises safety standards, there are areas in which there is no need to prove fault, such as nuisance, *Rylands* v *Fletcher* (1868) and under the principle of vicarious liability.

In criminal law, however, the desire to protect the blameless individual from the outcomes of state procedures and sanctions makes imposition of liability without fault less acceptable. Strict liability offences can only be created by the legislature in limited circumstances.

Examiner tip

Because you are required to write a balanced, two-sided essay it would be appropriate to pull your answer together in a conclusion, but the mark scheme is unlikely to require this specifically.

Meaning of fault — dictionary definitions 'thing wrongly done', 'responsibility for something wrong', 'culpable', 'blame'.

Areas of criminal law where the fault principle is important:

- *actus reus*:
  - act must be voluntary
  - omissions if a voluntary duty
  - responsibility for consequences
- *mens rea* — different levels of *mens rea*:
  - intention
  - oblique intent
  - subjective recklessness
- murder and voluntary manslaughter — both require intention to kill — defendant is less at fault if due to a loss of control or mental abnormality
- defences
- self-defence
- intoxication

Areas of criminal law where the fault principle is less clear:

- unlawful act manslaughter
- gross negligence manslaughter
- sections 47 and 20 Offences Against the Person Act 1861 *mens rea* does not equate with the harm caused

Aspects of criminal law which seem to reject the fault principle:

- motive not relevant, e.g. mercy killers have a good motive
- strict liability offences — no fault requirement in terms of *mens rea*
- absolute liability offences — no requirement of *mens rea* or that the act is voluntary
- mandatory sentences — do not reflect the differing levels of fault of defendants, e.g. murder and mercy killings

Aspects of tort where the fault principle is important:

- negligence — are they acting reasonably?
- occupiers' liability

- contributory negligence — fault of the victim reduces damages
- *volenti non fit injuria* — complete defence based on the victim's fault in voluntarily consenting to the risk of injury

Aspects of tort which seem to reject the fault principle:

- nuisance — reasonableness of the defendant not a defence, but motive and malice relevant, e.g. *Christie* v *Davey* (1893)
- *Rylands* v *Fletcher* strict liability for escape of things from defendant's land that cause damage; fault element introduced by *Cambridge Water Co.* case
- vicarious liability — lack of fault of employer is irrelevant
- Consumer Protection Act 1987 — imposes strict liability on producers for damage caused by defective products
- welfare state — some victims of work-related accidents can claim compensation from the state without need to prove fault

Arguments in favour of the requirement of fault in criminal law:

- effect of criminal sanctions and procedures
- strict liability is ineffective
- need to restrain state power
- strict liability can be unjust

Arguments in favour of the no-fault principle in criminal law:

- protection of the public
- saving of time and expense

Arguments in favour of the requirement of fault in tort:

- only those who are to blame should have to compensate the victim

Arguments in favour of the no-fault principle in tort:

- victims who cannot prove fault can be compensated

Balancing conflicting interests

Theorists

There are several important theorists who ought to be considered in the issue of balancing conflicting interests and whether the law is effective in achieving this.

Karl Marx

Karl Marx (1818–83) believed that law was part of the 'repressive state apparatus' used to ensure the continuing exploitation of the working class (proletariat) by the capitalists (bourgeoisie), i.e. those who own the capital and means of production. For Marx, the law subordinated the interests of the proletariat to those of the bourgeoisie and so did not truly balance conflicting interests. Marx adhered to the conflict model of society and thus was of the view that law did not reconcile conflicting interests in a compromise but rather imposed the interest of one at the expense of another.

Rudolf von Jhering

Rudolf von Jhering (1818–92) believed that the law was a prime method of ordering society. Von Jhering was a utilitarian and more concerned with social than individual aims. His thinking followed that of Jeremy Bentham, whose principle of utility was aimed at maximising human happiness by increasing pleasure and diminishing pain according to the principle of 'the greatest happiness of the greatest number'. He saw society as made up of several competing interests, not all of which could be satisfied. He believed that the interests of the individual would conflict with the interests of society as a whole. The role of the law was to balance interests by reconciling the interests of the individual to society so that they conformed. This was achieved through state-organised coercion, i.e. the law, rewards, duty and love.

Roscoe Pound

Roscoe Pound (1870–1964) divided interests into two main categories: individual interests and social interests. He argued that interests could only be properly balanced if placed on the same plane or level. Thus social interests can be weighed against social interests and individual interests against individual interests. Failure to do this results in a built-in bias in favour of the social interest. Pound thus developed the ideas of von Jhering. He saw law as being developed according to social needs and only serving those interests that lead to the good of society. He subscribed to the consensus model of society, believing interests should be balanced in accordance with society's values or 'jural postulates'.

> **Examiner tip**
> Balancing questions do not need as extensive a theoretical discussion as justice and morality questions, but it is useful to make brief reference to some of the ideas of people like Jhering and Pound.

The courts have not generally adopted Pound's approach For example, in *Miller* v *Jackson* (1977), involving an application for an injunction against a cricket club by residents whose properties adjoined the cricket ground, Lord Denning approached the problem in terms of 'a conflict between the interest of the public at large and the interests of a private individual'. Denning concluded that the public interest outweighed the individual interest and refused to grant the injunction, although he did attempt to balance this by awarding damages to compensate for the inconvenience of having cricket balls regularly hit into your garden.

Knowledge check 34

In *Miller* v *Jackson* what was the public interest and what was the private interest?

To have followed Pound would have necessitated seeing both interests in the same terms, either as individual interests (one person's desire to play cricket against another person's desire to sit in his/her garden) or as social interests (the value to society of protecting domestic privacy against the value of encouraging recreational activities).

Balancing of conflicting interests by Parliament

Legislative process

The balancing of competing interests is to some extent achieved by the process of making an Act of Parliament. The Green Paper invites consultation from various interested parties who may be affected by the proposed legislation. The bill stage of making the legislation requires many debates and votes. There are several political parties reflecting a wide range of views. Before the bill becomes an Act, many compromises and amendments will be made, which take into account the different views of those who are both interested and involved in the legislative process.

It is, however, questionable as to whether a true balance of conflicting interests is actually achieved by the legislative process. There are many powerful interest groups and classes within society. These groups influence the view of ministers, members of Parliament and civil servants. Many politicians are wealthy and influential. They may possess large shareholdings in companies and have directorships or other connections. They may be persuaded more often than they should by groups who are in favour of protecting such interests, despite requirements that these interests should be revealed.

Protective legislation

Parliament sometimes seeks to balance competing interests through legislation, which is advantageous to weaker interest groups. Examples of such protective legislation can be seen in consumer law. The **Consumer Protection Act 1987** imposes strict liability on producers in respect of damage caused by dangerous products. The **Sale and Supply of Goods Act 1994** applies conditions to consumer contracts in respect of title, description, quality and sale by sample. By virtue of the **Unfair Contract Terms Act 1977**, the use of exclusion and limitation clauses by businesses in consumer contracts is significantly reduced.

However Phil Harris, in *An Introduction to Law*, points out that such legislation is not rigorously enforced by the state, which results in the protective legislation aiding the stronger group while appearing to aid the weaker one. The perceived protection offered to consumers enables businesses to enjoy a better public image and so further their own interests.

A further problem with consumer legislation is that it depends on enforcement by the consumer. Harris believes that most consumers are ignorant of their legislative rights.

Legislation may also protect the individual from abuse by the state. The most obvious example is the **Human Rights Act**. A recent example is the **Protection of Freedoms Act 2012** which provides that the DNA of people arrested and charged but not convicted of a minor offence will no longer be kept and storage of the DNA of people arrested and charged but not convicted of a serious offence will be limited to 3 years. The Act also creates a surveillance camera commissioner to oversee the use of surveillance cameras. This is an issue of concern because, according to Liberal Democrat MP Tom Drake, under Labour Britain had 1% of the world's population and 20% of the world's surveillance cameras. Suspected terrorists are also given some protection through the reduction of the maximum period of detention without charge from 28 days to 14 days.

Decisions of government departments

In exercising their decision-making powers government departments are required to balance conflicting interests. Failure to consider the views of some interest groups or the public may result in perceived bias and embarrassing U-turns. In May 2012 the Department for Environment, Food and Rural affairs abandoned plans to take buzzards into captivity and destroy their nests to protect pheasant shoots. The U-turn followed an outcry from conservation groups and the public during which it was highlighted that the wildlife minister is a keen member of the shooting community.

Balancing of conflicting interests by the courts

Judges are more obviously faced with balancing competing interests in the courts, especially in areas such as nuisance, occupiers' liability, crime and consumer law:
- In nuisance, the claimant's interest in being able to enjoy his or her property must be balanced against the interest of his or her neighbours to do what they like with their property.
- In occupiers' liability, the interests of the occupier of land have to be balanced against the interests of people who come onto his or her land.
- In criminal law, the interests of the offender have to be balanced against the interests of society.
- In consumer law, the interests of the consumer have to be balanced against the interests of the business.

Public interests usually outweigh private interests

The public interest prevailed in May 2012 when Abu Qatada was refused bail pending his deportation appeal. While the decision was based on the high risk of Qatada absconding due to deportation being increasingly likely, Mr Justice Mitting referred

Knowledge check 35
Explain why protective legislation is needed.

Examiner tip
You are expected to explore a variety of ways in which the law seeks to achieve a balancing of conflicting interests. Better answers will consider law made by both the legislature and the decisions of the courts, and also the processes by which such laws are made. The actual interests that are being balanced should also be identified and weaker answers tend not to do this.

to 'the very high level of demand in resources' during the Olympics. The Home Office barrister had pointed out 'As a matter of logical inference, if Abu Qatada were to abscond, either resources would have to be diverted to finding him or finding him would have to be accorded a lower priority'.

The public interest also outweighs the private interest in respect of most positive rights provided by the European Convention on Human Rights and the **Human Rights Act 1998**. Most of these rights are subject to derogation clauses, which are sometimes drafted in broad terms. In *R (Begum)* v *Headteacher and Governors of Denbigh High School* (2006), Shabina Begum's claim that her right to practise her religion under Article 9 had been violated because the school's uniform policy prevented her wearing the jilbab was unsuccessful. The right to practise a religious belief is subject to limitations that are 'necessary in a democratic society for the protection of the rights and freedoms of others'. The interests of schools in devising uniform policies that are safe, inclusive and uncompetitive outweighs the interest of an individual in being able to wear what he or she wants.

The public interest has also prevailed in recent privacy cases involving celebrities. In April 2010 the *Sunday Mirror* published an article in which Carly Storey provided details of a 13-year affair with Rio Ferdinand, who was at the time the captain of the England football team and a married father. Carly Storey was paid £16,000 for the story. In *Rio Ferdinand* v *MGN Limited* (2011) Rio Ferdinand lost his claim for breach of privacy. The judge said 'it was a "kiss and paid for telling" story, but stories may be in the public interest even if the reasons behind the informant providing the information are less than noble...In the views of many, the captain was expected to maintain those standards off, as well as on, the pitch.'

Privacy cases require the courts to balance the public interest in freedom of expression and the private interest in privacy. There had been concern that celebrities were using Article 8 to protect their public image. However, the courts have moved towards protecting the public interest. In 2012 the European Court of Human Rights held that publication of photographs of Princess Caroline of Monaco and her husband on a skiing holiday alongside an article about the health of her father did not breach her right to privacy. On the question of balance the Joint Committee on Privacy and Injunctions concluded 'We believe that the courts are now striking a better balance between the right to privacy and the right to freedom of expression, based on the facts of the individual case.'

Knowledge check 36

What public interest is considered in privacy cases brought by celebrities against newspapers?

Private interests do sometimes outweigh public interests

Under Article 8 of the European Convention on Human Rights, everyone has the right to respect for his or her private and family life, home and correspondence. However, Article 8 also expressly provides that this right can be overridden 'in the interests of national security, public safety or the economic well-being of the country, for the prevention of disorder or crime, for the protection of health or morals, or for the protection of the rights and freedoms of others'. Thus it seems the rights of individuals will not prevail in the event of a conflict with the public interest. However in *Mosley* v *News Group Newspapers Ltd* (2008), the private interest of the claimant did prevail. This decision provoked an angry response from the editor of the *Daily Mail*, who viewed the decision as an attack on freedom of expression. The private interest under Article 8 also prevailed in *Dickson* v *UK* (2007). The private interest of a prisoner serving life for murder to be able to artificially inseminate a woman he had married since starting his prison sentence prevailed over the public interest in maintaining confidence in the prison system. In *Marper* (2008) the EctHR also found in favour of the private interest and held that storing the DNA of innocent people failed to strike a fair balance between the competing public and private interests and accordingly constituted a breach of Article 8.

A and others v *Secretary of State for the Home Department* (2004) provides another example of the courts deciding in favour of the private interest. The House of Lords decided that the use of s.21 of the **Anti-Terrorism, Crime and Security Act 2001** to detain foreign nationals without charging them was unlawful and an infringement of their human rights. Despite the public interest arguments put forward by the home secretary, the Law Lords were willing to recognise the importance of preserving private interests.

While even the right to life is subject to qualification, some rights, including the right not to be subjected to torture or to inhuman or degrading treatment or punishment (Article 3), are non-derogable and thus ensure that an individual interest cannot be outweighed by a public interest.

Jurors are not part of the permanent state machinery of enforcement. Perhaps, as a result, they are more willing than judges to question claims made by the executive or legislature of threats to national security. In *R* v *Ponting* (1985), a civil servant was charged under the **Official Secrets Act 1911** for leaking information about the sinking of the *Belgrano*, an Argentinian ship, during the Falklands War. Ponting argued that leaking the information was in the public interest because it showed that the British government had not been telling the truth. The judge said that Ponting's argument was no defence. The jury took a different view and acquitted him.

National interests and local interests

Sometimes the courts are willing to reject the idea that the national interest should outweigh the local interest. In May 2012 a proposal to build four 100-metre turbines in a beauty spot on the edge of the Norfolk Broads was rejected by the High Court. Mrs Justice Lang said: 'As a matter of law it is not correct to assert that the national policy promoting the use of renewable resources…negates the local landscape policies or must be given primacy over them.'

It is likely that other disputes involving planning issues will occur in the future and it is interesting to speculate in this context on the impact that the **Localism Act 2011** might have. Greg Clark, the Minister of State for Communities and Local Government, described the Act as providing 'a major turning point in the balance of power in this country as new rights and freedoms for communities to take back control come into force'. However, critics have argued that the Act, by making assumptions in favour of 'sustainable development', will make it easier for developers to push development projects through.

> **Examiner tip**
>
> Examples of balancing can be found in every part of substantive law. In this section we explore a few, but many others could be used instead. For example, in the law of contract areas that might be considered are balancing the interests of the offeror and the offeree, achieving the right balance when deciding on appropriate remedies, and achieving balance when a contract is frustrated.

The civil courts and access to justice

Interests can only be balanced if there are institutions available to which aggrieved parties have access on an equal basis. The operation of the rule of law, state-assisted funding of legal actions and the independence of the judiciary ensure that, in theory at least, the court and tribunal system is able to achieve balance.

However, the findings of the Woolf commission (cost, delay and complexity) provide ample evidence that the civil courts often operate in ways which favour powerful organisations and disadvantage individual claimants. It could be argued that tribunals provide a fairer balance in that they have fewer formal procedures and encourage claimants to represent themselves. However, no government funding is available and the ordinary claimant is likely to be facing an opponent who is represented, e.g. an employer or a government department, and this puts him or her at a significant disadvantage.

The small claims procedure is also designed to achieve greater balance between the parties and, as with the tribunal system, the emphasis is on informality. But again, there is evidence that the balance remains in favour of the parties who can afford to use lawyers. The majority of cases are brought by businesses trying to recover bad debts rather than by individual claimants. Clearly the **Legal Aid (Sentencing and Punishment of Offenders) Act 2012** which aims to reduce the public funding budget by £350 million will prevent access to justice and thus prevent interests being balanced by the courts. As we saw in the previous section, many areas of law have been removed from funding and the financial limit for cases being directed to the small claims court, for which no funding is available for legal representation, has been increased from £5,000 to £10,000 with a view to it being increased to £15,000.

> **Knowledge check 37**
>
> Why does a lack of government funding for legal advice and representation prevent a balancing of conflicting interests?

Balancing conflicting interests in criminal law

Criminal law is concerned with balancing the interests of the offender with those of society. This can be evidenced both in criminal procedure and in the substantive criminal law.

Criminal procedure

The interest of society is the conviction of the guilty and the acquittal of the innocent. The interest of the defendant is to have an assumption of innocence, to be treated with dignity and to have a fair trial. There is also the interest of the victim to consider. The traditional balance of the law in favour of the defendant may leave victims feeling that their interests are not being effectively represented in the criminal process.

There are many aspects that could be considered here and much specific detail can be drawn from Unit 1. Of particular importance are the **Criminal Procedure and Investigation Act 1996**, which allows for the retrial of someone acquitted by a jury where there is evidence of intimidation of witnesses, and the **Criminal Justice Act**

2003 (CJA), which gives the Court of Appeal the power to order a retrial where 'new and compelling evidence' comes to light after someone has been found not guilty.

In addition, there is the whole issue that surrounds the rights of defendants — burden of proof, rules on arrest, rules of evidence, right to silence, effect of not-guilty finding — and how these rules are designed to create balance between the prosecution and the defence. It is important to address the question of whether the balance has now swung too far in favour of the prosecution, and to look at the right to silence and the effect of s.34 of the **Criminal Justice and Public Order Act 1994 (CJPOA)**, which allow juries or magistrates to draw inferences from a defendant failing to mention, when under caution, facts later relied on in his defence — an issue highlighted by the Court of Appeal in the *Sam Hallam* case. Another example is the issue of whether an accused person should be entitled to bail. The **Bail Act 1976** created a presumption in favour of bail. The courts are obliged to grant bail unless one of the exceptions applies. This Act seeks to ensure the liberty of the accused until the trial. The court has to balance the interest of the public in being protected and the interest of the individual in being presumed innocent until proven guilty. There had been a shift towards the public interest in recent years, with legislation increasingly providing circumstances in which bail may or must be refused. However, the **Legal Aid (Sentencing and Punishment of Offenders) Act 2012** appears to reverse that trend. In what has been suggested is an attempt to cut the number of people held in custody, the Act provides that people awaiting trial will now be granted bail where there is no real prospect of them receiving a custodial sentence upon conviction, although the Act does allow prosecutors to appeal against Crown Court bail decisions.

The Act also abolishes Indeterminate Sentences for Public Protection (IPPs) introduced by the **Criminal Justice Act 2003** which provided for the detention of offenders who had served their sentences but who, in the court's opinion, posed a significant risk to the public of serious harm by the commission of further specified offences. IPPs were widely used. In 2008, 1,468 were issued and the number of prisoners serving IPPs was 4,461. Only 4% of IPP prisoners have ever been released. However, the Act stops short of providing for the release of current IPP prisoners. While appealing to the interests of the defendant the 2012 Act contains measures to protect the interests of the victim.

The secretary of state is also given new powers under the Act to make rules about prisoners' employment, pay and deductions from their pay. The intention is that such rules will provide for prisoners making payments which support victims of crime. This can be seen as a further attempt to redress the balance between defendant and victim.

> **Knowledge check 38**
>
> What are the three interests to be considered in criminal cases?

Substantive criminal law: the defence of intoxication

The public interest lies in being protected from those who cause harm when drunk. The individual interest lies in being held less responsible for actions carried out while intoxicated (and thus with limited *mens rea*) than for actions carried out with full awareness.

The availability of the defence of intoxication varies according to circumstances. Where the accused is involuntarily intoxicated, intoxication can be a defence to any crime, provided the accused lacks the necessary *mens rea*. Voluntary intoxication, however, can only be a defence to a crime of specific intent. The courts regard voluntary intoxication as reckless in itself and recklessness is the level of *mens rea* required for crimes of basic intent. In *DPP* v *Majewski* (1977), the House of Lords refused to allow voluntary intoxication to be used as a defence to a basic intent offence. Lord Steyn said that one of the prime purposes of the criminal law is the protection from unprovoked violence of people who are pursuing their lawful lives; to allow intoxication as a defence would be to leave the citizen unprotected from such violence. The House of Lords was of the opinion that to allow voluntary intoxication as a defence would not provide a proper balance between the interests of the defendant and the interests of society as a whole.

The concept of strict liability

In the creation of strict liability crimes, the law may suppress the interests of the individual in the interest of public safety. The **Rivers (Prevention of Pollution) Act 1951** makes it a criminal offence to pollute rivers, without the need to prove that such pollution is caused intentionally, recklessly or negligently. In *Alphacell* v *Woodward* (1972) the defendants were found guilty of polluting a river, despite the fact that they were not negligent and were unaware of the mechanical breakdown of their equipment, which usually prevented such pollution occurring. One justification for strict liability in situations like this is that it works to the disadvantage of the more powerful interest and thus helps to achieve balance.

> **Knowledge check 39**
>
> What public interest is protected by strict liability offences?

Balancing conflicting interests in the law of tort

The law of tort is mainly concerned with balancing two individual interests. However, public interests sometimes arise, as seen earlier when considering *Miller* v *Jackson* (1977). In that case, the public interest was considered when determining whether to award an injunction.

Negligence

The interest of one individual in not being harmed through another's carelessness has to be balanced against the interest of the other individual in not being held liable for unforeseeable and remote consequences. Limiting the number of potential claimants is also necessary because ultimately an insurance company will pay the compensation and insurance premiums have to be kept to an affordable level.

In the law on psychiatric injury, the law limits liability to secondary victims by applying stringent criteria not applied to primary victims. Primary victims, e.g. those directly involved in an accident, can clearly be foreseen as being likely to be affected by the defendant's actions. However, the courts apply restrictions on who can claim as a result of seeing or hearing something happen to someone else.

It was made clear in *Alcock* v *Chief Constable of South Yorkshire* (1991) and *Page* v *Smith* (1995) that a secondary victim must prove five additional criteria:

(1) he or she is a person of ordinary phlegm
(2) he or she has close ties of love and affection with those in the accident
(3) he or she is close in time and space
(4) he or she perceived the accident with his or her own unaided senses
(5) it can be shown that psychiatric illness rather than just physical injury was foreseeable

Whether a true balancing of conflicting interests is achieved by these criteria is questionable. The trauma of a person identifying a body in a mortuary or seeing an accident on television could be just as great as a qualifying claimant, but the court has to consider the interests of the defendant as well. It is arguably not fair to allow claims from people not directly involved in the accident, unless they are foreseeable claimants.

Knowledge check 40

What public interest is protected by limiting the number of people who can claim in negligence?

Nuisance

The law of private nuisance is concerned with balancing the competing interests of neighbours to enjoy their property. Any interference which is unreasonable is unlawful. In deciding whether the level of interference is unreasonable, the courts take into account factors such as locality, sensitivity and malice. For example in *Laws* v *Florinplace Ltd* (1981), when a shop in a residential area was converted into a sex shop and cinema club, locality was a relevant factor, and in *Hollywood Silver Fox Farm* v *Emmett* (1936), the claim succeeded because the defendant had deliberately set out to cause harm.

Conclusion

It is clear that there is an attempt to balance conflicting interests both in the creation of legislation and in the courts.

The consultation process and bill stage of making legislation ensure that a range of interests is at least considered, but it is questionable whether a true balancing of conflicting interests is achieved due to the influence of powerful and wealthy interest groups. In civil law, an attempt is made to strengthen the weaker party through protective legislation. However, the effectiveness of this legislation is reliant on individuals having the knowledge, tenacity, financial means and time to enforce their rights. In criminal law, legislative developments concerning criminal procedure appear to place greater importance on the interests of society and the victims of crime.

In the courts, judges can be seen to attempt a balancing of conflicting interests both in the decision and in the remedy/sanction. While there are some exceptions, judges arguably continue to favour the public interest over the private interest. For example, the law relating to psychiatric injury has clearly been developed based on policy — to limit the number of claims being brought before the courts and to keep insurance premiums to affordable levels. The same can be said regarding the refusal of the House of Lords to allow voluntary intoxication as a defence to crimes of basic intent.

Examiner tip

A good answer, as well as identifying appropriate issues, the interests to be balanced and the ways in which the law tries to achieve balance, will evaluate how effectively balance is achieved. In mark schemes this will probably constitute potential content B and discussion of the effectiveness of the balance should therefore form an important part of your answer.

Summary

Theorists:

- Marx — conflict model, one interest imposed (bourgeoisie) at expense of another (proletariat)
- Jhering — utilitarian, greatest happiness of greatest number, reconcile interests of individual to society
- Pound — balance interests on same level, private vs private, public vs public, conflict with *Miller* v *Jackson*

Balancing of conflicting interests by Parliament:

- legislative process — debates, votes, but influence of powerful groups, legislators' interests
- protective legislation, e.g. consumer law, but dependent on individual enforcement, Human Rights Act, Protection of Freedoms Act 2012
- decisions of government departments should consider all interests, e.g. plans to reduce buzzards U-turn 2012

Balancing of conflicting interests by the courts:

- Many areas of law require courts to balance competing interests, e.g. nuisance, occupiers' liability, crime, consumer law.
- Public interests often outweigh private interests, e.g. Qatada refused bail 2012; derogation clauses in Human Rights Act, e.g. Begum (2006), Ferdinand case (2011).
- Private interests sometimes outweigh public interests, e.g. *Mosley* v *NGN* (2008), *Marper* (2008), *A & others* (2004), Article 3 non-derogable.
- Local interests can prevail over national interests, e.g. rejection of wind turbines Norfolk Broads 2012.
- Equal access to civil justice denied through cuts in government funding, e.g. Legal Aid (SPO) Act 2012.

Balancing conflicting interests in criminal law:

- Interests of society — conviction of the guilty, acquittal of the innocent. Interests of defendant — assumption of innocence, dignified treatment, fair trial.
- Criminal procedure — retrials following acquittal when witnesses intimidated, and when new and compelling evidence. CJA 2003 favours public interest, as does weakening right to silence, CJPOA 1994, highlighted in *Sam Hallam* case. Legal Aid (SPO) Act 2012 no real prospect test and abolition of IPPs favour interests of defendant; deductions from prisoners' pay to support victims recognises interests of victims.
- Substantive criminal law: intoxication. Public interest — protection from drunk people causing harm; individual interest — being less responsible for acts done without full awareness. Voluntary intoxication no defence to basic intent crimes — would not provide balance between interests of defendant and interests of society, e.g. *Majewski*.
- Strict liability offences — individual interest subordinated to public interest, e.g. public safety, *Alphacell* v *Woodward* (1972).

Balancing conflicting interests in tort:

- Negligence — individual interest in not being harmed vs individual interest in not being liable for unforeseeable consequences, e.g. limited liability to secondary victims (e.g. *Alcock*, *Page* v *Smith*); also public interest in affordable insurance.
- Nuisance — balances competing individual interests of neighbours, unreasonable interference unlawful, e.g. *Miller* v *Jackson*, damages awarded, injunction not in public interest.

Questions & Answers

How to use this section

This section provides you with five questions, which cover all the Unit 4 (Section C) Concepts of Law areas. In this examination paper, all the questions are set as essays and they are not subdivided.

There will be a choice of three questions, of which you must answer one. Students are required to write a continuous piece of prose. However, the questions do usually ask students to consider more than one aspect, and the A-grade answers provided in this section should give you a clear idea of the approach and structure required.

Remember that despite the allocation of 30 marks to this question, you are, as stated in the AQA specification, expected to write 'an hour-long essay'.

Examples and supporting evidence for questions in Unit 4 (Section C) Concepts of Law can be taken from anywhere across the whole AS and A2 specifications. You will notice that some of the answers in this section follow the material used in this guide quite closely. However, it would be possible to write A-grade answers to each of the questions using entirely different material. What matters in Unit 4 (Section C) Concepts of Law answers is how the material is used and how it relates to the ideas in the question.

Each question is followed by an A-grade answer.

To acquire the necessary skills and become more familiar with this style of examination question, it is a good idea to practise adapting the A-grade answers for different questions. You are strongly encouraged to download past papers and mark schemes from AQA (www.aqa.org.uk) or to obtain these from your teacher.

Examiner's comments

Each question is followed by a brief analysis of what to watch out for when answering it (shown by the icon ⓔ). The student answers are accompanied by examiner's comments (preceded by the icon ⓔ). These help explain the elements of the answer for which marks can be awarded and are intended to give you an insight into what examiners are looking for.

Question 1 Law and morality

Discuss the relationship between law and morals and consider whether the debate on the relationship is still relevant.

(30 marks)

ⓔ This question requires you to 'discuss'. This means that you must present arguments and make comments about the relationship. In considering whether the debate is still relevant your task is to explain the nature of the Hart–Devlin debate and the views that were held and then to discuss whether there is evidence that the views presented in that debate are still relevant.

A-grade answer

Law is best described as rules made by authority. John Austin defined law as a command from a sovereign power. Law needs to be obeyed and is enforced through various sanctions. Morality is really values and principles rather than rules. Phil Harris defines a society's 'code of morality' as a set of 'beliefs, values, principles and standards of behaviour'. Compliance is voluntary, though society can enforce moral codes informally, for example through disapproval and social rejection.

There are a number of clear distinctions between law and morality. For example, law can always be proved by referring to the written record of it, whereas morality is opinion and open to dispute. Second, law can change instantly, for example homosexuality was legalised when the Sexual Offences Act 1967 came into effect and the ban on smoking in public places came into force on 1 July 2007. Morality on the other hand changes gradually. Finally, the sanctions for breaking the law are severe and could involve financial penalties or loss of liberty, while sanctions for breaking moral rules are usually social.

But law and morality can also overlap. Sir John Salmond illustrated this by referring to overlapping circles. For example, there are many long-established legal rules that have a moral connection. These include the laws of murder and theft, which can be traced back to the Ten Commandments. For example, the Christian Bible and Jewish Torah state 'You shall not steal' and clearly the Theft Acts reflect this moral assertion. Also, changing moral views can lead to changes in the law. The legalisation of homosexuality and the banning of corporal punishment in schools are good examples of issues where general public attitudes had gradually changed and then the law changed, in part as a response to changed moral views. But the law can also be changed by judges. The case of *R* v *R* is a good example of the courts recognising that public morality had changed and deciding as a result that the previous legal position that a man could not be charged with raping his wife was no longer acceptable.

ⓔ The answer begins with brief definitions and then explores the distinctions and the overlap between law and morality, using a range of examples. The answer goes on to discuss the difficulties the law has with following morality, which is an important aspect of the relationship.

In practice it is often difficult for law to follow morality. Britain is becoming more pluralistic and this means that there are more likely to be disagreements about what is morally right for the law to do. There are a number of issues on which there are conflicting moral views, which are very strongly held. Perhaps the most obvious of these is abortion. Despite the passing of the Abortion Act in 1967 the issue remains contentious. In the debates leading up to the passing of the Human Fertilisation and Embryology Act 2008 190 MPs voted in favour of reducing the current 24-week abortion limit and some favoured a reduction to 12 weeks. But others argued passionately for the current limit to remain. Assisted suicide is another issue that has generated passionate debate.

In the 1960s there was an important debate about the role morality should have in the making of law. It was called the Hart–Devlin debate and it arose out of the Wolfenden Report which recommended that homosexuality should be legalised. Devlin's view was that it should not be legalised because it was important that the law should enforce the existing morality of the nation, otherwise there was a risk of society disintegrating. Lord Devlin's views are reflective of the late nineteenth-century criminal judge Sir James Stephen and of earlier natural law theorists like Aquinas. Devlin believed that the law should punish acts which offend the common morality, whether done in public or in private.

Hart's view was the opposite. He said that to use the law to enforce morality was 'unnecessary, undesirable and unacceptable' and would freeze morality at a particular point and prevent change. Professor Hart drew on the work of John Stuart Mill and the positivists who had argued that the only part of someone's behaviour that should concern society is that which affects others: 'Over himself, over his own body and mind, the individual is sovereign'.

ⓔ It is important in the second part of the essay that the Hart–Devlin debate is explained and discussed. This answer also refers briefly to the theorists who influenced Professor Hart and Lord Devlin so that they are placed in a wider context.

The immediate result of the debate was that Hart's view was adopted and homosexuality was legalised. Other examples of his view being followed were the Obscene Publications Act 1968 and the Divorce Law Reform Act 1969. However, there are many examples of Devlin's view being followed. Cases like *Brown*, *Shaw* and *Leach* all show that judges were making legal decisions based on maintaining moral standards.

The case of *Gillick* illustrates both views being applied. Three of the five House of Lords judges followed the Hart view and decided that girls under 16 should be able to get contraceptive advice without their parents' consent and make their own decisions about their own bodies. The two dissenting judges argued the Devlin view that it was important to uphold existing moral standards.

In lots of ways this debate is still relevant. Aspects of gay rights still cause divisions of opinion just like those of Hart–Devlin. For example, the Catholic Adoption Agency was prevented from operating because it refused to put children with gay couples and several individual Christians have lost cases because of their views on homosexuality. For example, Eunice and Owen Johns were stopped from fostering and in *Bull & Bull* v *Hall & Preddy* the Court upheld the entitlement of gay couples in civil partnerships to shared accommodation in hotels and guest houses. This was followed by the case brought by Black and Morgan against the Christian owners of a B & B who would not let them share a bed.

Although the Civil Partnership Act 2004 gives same-sex couples the same legal entitlements as marriage there is currently a fierce argument about whether the law should be further changed to allow gay marriage. Once again Christians, in particular both Anglican and Roman Catholic bishops, have spoken out strongly against this, while many politicians including both the prime minister and the deputy prime minister have expressed support for it.

Also there are ethical issues where there is the same difference of opinion. For example, in both abortion and euthanasia there is disagreement between those who argue that human life is sacred (clearly a moral view and similar to that of Devlin) and those who say that religious people should not impose their views on those who want to act differently (the Hart view).

In conclusion we can see that the relationship between law and morality is complex and the debate on that relationship continues to be relevant.

(e) The remainder of the essay looks at the evidence for the continuing importance of the debate. It explores the impact of the debate on legislation and judicial decisions in the immediate aftermath and then goes on to look at current issues. Notice that a range of issues are considered and the answer clearly attempts to refer to events that were in the news at the time of writing.

(e) **29 or 30/30 marks awarded.** This is a clearly structured and well-argued essay. It uses a range of examples, which are relevant to the points being made. Both parts of the question are fully covered and would be assessed as sound.

Question 2 **Law and justice**

Discuss the meaning of justice and consider whether justice is achieved in Britain. (30 marks)

(e) This question asks you to 'discuss' and 'consider'. Both these terms require you to present arguments and to comment critically.

A-grade answer

Justice is not the same as law. Laws are rules, which must be obeyed by everyone in society. They are rules made with authority and they are created and enforced by the state. Justice is about fairness, the idea that people should be treated in the same way, though as Perelman points out it is not always just to treat people in the same way. For example, it would not be fair always to give people identical sentences for the same offence because that would take no account of mitigating or aggravating factors.

Sir John Salmond defined justice as based on two main ideas: substantive justice — the rules must be fair in themselves; formal/procedural justice — the rules must be applied in a fair way.

ⓔ The question asks you to discuss the meaning of justice, which this answer does quite briefly.

There are many theories about justice. The Greek philosopher Aristotle, for example, identified two types of justice. Distributive justice is the allocation of assets, such as wealth and honour, in a proportionate way, not based on equal shares but based on the contribution made by each individual. Corrective justice applies when distributive justice is interrupted by wrongdoing and involves punishing the offender and giving compensation to the victim.

Natural law theory is based on the idea that there is a higher order of law and if society follows this order, then it will be just. St Thomas Aquinas said that this came from God and he argued that if a law conflicted with natural law, it need not be obeyed. But natural law theory is not always based on religious belief. Professor Lon Fuller refers to what he terms the 'inner morality of law' which would form the basis of justice.

According to utilitarianism, put forward by J. S. Mill and Jeremy Bentham, society should work towards the greatest happiness for the greatest number, even if some individuals lose out. This means that as long as a law results in greater happiness for the majority then it is just, even if it results in social inequality.

Karl Marx believed that it was impossible for a capitalist society to be just as the laws are made to uphold the interests of the ruling class. In contrast Nozick argued that the redistribution of wealth demanded by Marx would be fundamentally unfair and that a society could only be just if people were free to enjoy their wealth without state interference.

John Rawls believed that justice could only be achieved by placing people in the original position behind a veil of ignorance. The system chosen by these people would be just. This is because these people would not know what their position would be in the system they were creating. They would thus choose rules giving everyone the right to the most extensive basic liberty compatible with a similar liberty for others and would only allow social and economic inequalities which were of benefit to all and attached to positions open to all. This idea of justice is one that many people in modern liberal democracies would accept and it seems to address the criticisms that could be made of the utilitarian view and the arguments of Marx and Nozick.

ⓔ This section considers various theories on the meaning of justice at much greater length.

It could be argued that the position in Britain fulfils the criteria that Rawls sets out at least in respect of guaranteeing fundamental rights and freedoms. Both the rule of law and natural justice operate and any decisions of the government can be challenged through judicial review conducted by an independent judiciary. Basic rights are safeguarded by the Human Rights Act and there are many examples of the government losing human rights cases, for example *A and others* v *Home Secretary*, which concerned the issue of detaining suspected foreign terrorists without charging them. Even in situations like that in the Pinochet case, where the rules of natural justice appeared not to have been applied, the system allows for mistakes to be put right and injustices corrected.

However, while it could be argued that substantive justice is achieved because the basic rules are fundamentally fair, there are many examples where there appears to be a lack of procedural justice and corrective justice.

Particularly in the 1980s and 1990s there were a number of miscarriages of justice like the Bridgwater Four, who served many years in prison and one defendant actually died in prison, before it was proved that there were things wrong with the investigation. Other cases include the Tottenham Three and the Birmingham Six. In all these cases it was eventually accepted, long after the convictions and after unsuccessful appeals, that there were concerns about the reliability of forensic evidence and the treatment of the defendants in custody.

The Stephen Lawrence case in particular highlights the fact that while the rules might be fundamentally fair they are not always implemented fairly. Although two men have now been convicted of Lawrence's murder, the police failed to investigate the case properly and were accused by the Macpherson Inquiry of institutional racism. There are now concerns that corrupt police officers may have obstructed the original investigation.

Another issue that may prevent some individuals receiving justice is that of expert evidence in criminal trials. Increasingly cases are turning on highly technical forensic evidence and juries have to rely on the views of expert witnesses. The testimony of the eminent paediatrician Professor Sir Roy Meadow, which was later discredited, led to the conviction of several 'cot death mothers' including Sally Clarke and Angela Cannings, even though in these cases there was no forensic evidence to justify convictions. A recent case where potential injustice also arose because of mistaken judgements by doctors is that of Rohan Wray and Chana Al-Alas who were accused of murdering their baby because doctors failed to diagnose that in fact he had died of rickets.

ⓔ The second part of the essay requires you to consider whether justice is achieved. This answer deals with this first by considering whether substantive justice is achieved and then by looking at various examples of miscarriages of justice.

Juries illustrate very well the difficulty in ensuring that corrective justice is achieved. Most people would argue that juries are fundamental in ensuring justice. They are the lamp that shows that freedom lives and they allow ordinary people to exercise independent justice without fear of state interference as illustrated by the jury decision in *Ponting*.

However, as the Roskill Commission said, juries may have difficulty understanding complex fraud cases and may acquit someone wrongly, creating injustice for the victim. Jury nobbling with bribes or threats could also affect jury decisions and make them unfair. As a result the Criminal Justice Act 2003 allows trial by a judge without a jury if there is a real danger of jury nobbling. In *R* v *Twomey* in January 2010 the defendants were convicted of serious offences after a trial without a jury and after three previous jury trials, the last one having been abandoned due to jury nobbling.

Another potential source of injustice is the increasing use of modern technology by jurors. In January 2012, Theodora Dallas researched a defendant's past on the internet and shared the information with fellow jury members The Court of Appeal jailed her and said that 'the damage to the administration of justice is obvious'. In June 2011,

Joanne Fraill was jailed after using Facebook while on a jury to exchange messages with a defendant.

Also, although juries are picked at random, they can still have prejudices and it seems very difficult to avoid this especially in high-profile cases reported in the media. However, the conclusions of the Thomas Report in 2010 suggest that juries seem remarkably free from racial prejudice at least. They found that conviction rates for white and Asian defendants were identical and those for black defendants only slightly higher. They also found that all white juries did not discriminate against ethnic minority defendants.

In conclusion we can see that the achievement of justice is not always easy. Although the fundamental rules seem to be fair there are often problems with the way corrective justice works in practice.

(e) The last part of the answer looks at the role played by juries in the achievement of justice. Notice how the answer discusses both the strengths of the jury system and also the ways in which it might make the achievement of justice difficult.

(e) **29 or 30/30 marks awarded.** This is a balanced answer which addresses both parts of the question. It is a genuine discussion and the arguments are supported by relevant and well-explained examples.

Question 3 Judicial creativity

Referring to precedent and statutory interpretation, discuss how creative judges can be, and compare their contribution to the development of the law with that of Parliament.   (30 marks)

(e) This question requires a discussion. This means that you must develop arguments and make comments, rather than just describe how judges can be creative.

A-grade answer

The constitutional role of the judiciary is to apply the law that Parliament makes. However, judges are able to create law through precedent and statutory interpretation.

The doctrine of precedent requires judges to follow decisions made in earlier cases and appears to limit their freedom to be creative. Lower courts are bound by the decisions of higher courts, the Court of Appeal, despite Lord Denning's efforts to free it, is bound by its own decisions, and the legal reason for the decision must be followed by later courts in cases concerning similar facts.

However, judges are able to exercise considerable creativity. In some areas of law (e.g. contract, negligence and fatal offences), judges make nearly all the legal rules. *Donoghue* v *Stevenson* was a very creative judgement which established the modern law of negligence.

The Practice Direction in theory gives the House of Lords almost unlimited power to change earlier precedent. It has used it to bring about significant changes in the law, for example that duress cannot be used as a defence to murder (*R* v *Howe*, 1987) and that the *mens rea* of recklessness is subjective (*R* v *G*, 2003).

When there is no precedent judges can use legal reasoning and persuasive precedents to be creative. The law on negligent misstatement was developed from the dissenting judgement of Lord Denning in *Candler* v *Crane Christmas* (1951). In *R (Guardian News and Media Limited)* v *City of Westminster Magistrates' Court* (2012) the Court of Appeal held that access should be permitted to documents which have been placed before and referred to in open proceedings. Lord Justice Toulson acknowledged the strong persuasive authority of decisions of superior courts in Canada, New Zealand and South Africa which were referred to in the case. Judges can also distinguish the case from the precedent when the facts are materially different. *Merritt* v *Merritt* did not follow the decision in *Balfour* v *Balfour* because in the later case the couple were separated. Higher courts can reverse the decisions of lower courts in appeal cases (e.g. *Tomlinson* v *Congleton BC*) and can overrule earlier precedents by lower courts.

ⓔ The question refers specifically to precedent and the answer begins by considering the ways in which precedent allows and limits judicial law-making.

When interpreting statutes judges explain ambiguous and unclear wording. They also interpret clear words or phrases that seem to go against commonsense or the spirit of the Act. They have aids to help them, which allow some creativity. For example, they can refer to other parts of the Act or to a report (e.g. by the Law Commission) on which the Act was based. In *Pepper* v *Hart* (1993) it was held *Hansard* can, in certain circumstances, be referred to.

Using the mischief rule/purposive approach sometimes changes the clear meaning of words. Supporters of the literal rule, such as Viscount Simmonds, say this usurps the role of Parliament. Creative judges like Lord Denning argue it is the duty of the court to fill in the gaps and look for what Parliament intended to say. In *Royal College of Nursing* v *DHSS*, the words 'by a registered medical practitioner' were changed to 'under the supervision of...' to promote the intention of Parliament to provide access to safe legal abortion. The purposive approach allows a broader interpretation of a word or phrase than the literal rule. In *R* v *Cockburn* (2008), the Court of Appeal upheld the defendant's conviction under the Offences Against the Person Act of 'setting a mantrap or other engine...with intent to cause grievous bodily harm'. Using the purposive approach it held that a spiked metal object attached to the roof of a shed so that it would fall on anyone opening the shed door was an engine. Increasing use of the purposive approach is partly due to the influence of European Union law, which is drafted in general terms assuming judges will fill in the detail. Also influential is the Human Rights Act, which allows judges to consider whether an Act complies with the European Convention on Human Rights.

Judges using the literal rule are less creative and sometimes justify absurd decisions by reference to parliamentary sovereignty. In *Fisher* v *Bell* a knife in a shop window was not being 'offered' for sale, because displays of goods in shop windows are invitations to treat. Applying the literal rule, the defendant was not guilty. In the judge's view it was the role of Parliament, not the court, to amend the Act.

Judges can use the 'golden rule', where the wording creates an absurd or repugnant situation (e.g. *Sigsworth*, where literal interpretation of the Act would allow a man to inherit from his mother, whom he had murdered).

(e) The answer goes on, as the question requires, to consider the scope judges have to be creative through statutory interpretation.

Compared to judges it would seem Parliament can be much more creative for several reasons. It can choose when to legislate and can conduct comprehensive research. Judges have to wait for a suitable case to be brought and can only consider evidence presented during the case. They cannot consider wider aspects, even though their decision (e.g. *Gillick*) may have implications for society generally.

Unlike Parliament judges can only make law on the facts before them. Small changes, such as the reintroduction of gross negligence manslaughter in *Prentice/Adomako*, do not help when the whole area needs reforming. Also, judge-made law operates retrospectively. The decision in *R* v *R* (1991) turned an act that was lawful at the time it was committed into a serious criminal offence. The European Court of Human Rights upheld the decision on the basis that judicial law-making was well entrenched in legal tradition and development of the law on this issue had been foreseeable. In *R* v *Crooks* (2004) the Court of Appeal upheld the conviction of a man who had intercourse with his wife without her consent 32 years before his conviction and 21 years before the *R* v *R* decision.

The House of Lords uses the Practice Direction sparingly (e.g. in *Knuller* it would not overrule *Shaw*), because changing the law frequently causes uncertainty. Many judges prefer to leave reform of the criminal law, where certainty is particularly important, to Parliament. Rejecting an appeal by Debbie Purdy, who had wanted the law clarified to enable her husband to assist her suicide without fear of prosecution, Lord Judge in the Court of Appeal in 2009 said: 'It is no part of the court's function to enter into that debate. The proper forum for that discussion is Parliament.' The decision was overturned in the House of Lords later that year.

However, in many areas Parliament has chosen not to legislate and increasingly has less time for law reform. The report of the Joint Committee on Privacy and Injunctions in 2012 shows preference for judicial reform of the law of privacy. Judicial law-making is not anti-democratic because Parliament can overrule their decisions.

(e) The question also requires a comparison of the law-making role of judges with that of Parliament and the answer does this very effectively.

In conclusion, it appears that judges can be creative, but that they are and should be less creative than Parliament. Nevertheless they are adopting an increasingly creative role due to the influence of the European Union and the Human Rights Act.

(e) **29 or 30/30 marks awarded.** This is a balanced and clear answer, packed with relevant examples from several parts of the specification. It deals with all the aspects of the question and is clearly structured and systematic. One of its strengths is that it never becomes a purely descriptive answer. It frequently refers back to the question and makes appropriate analytical comments.

Question 4 Fault

'Establishing liability based on fault is regarded as a fundamental principle of English law.'
Discuss the arguments in support of and against this view.

(30 marks)

ⓔ A variety of command words may be used in the questions on this paper. This question asks you to 'discuss the arguments'. Questions will sometimes ask you to 'explain and evaluate'. In each case the requirement is to present arguments with supporting evidence and to comment critically. Examiners are always looking for more than a simple listing of arguments and often the wording of the question will be subtly different from those in previous exams, requiring students to consider the issue in a slightly different way.

A-grade answer

Fault is the idea that a person is responsible for his or her actions and that in some way he or she has behaved wrongly. There are various definitions of the word 'fault'. The *Concise Oxford Dictionary* defines it as a 'thing wrongly done' and 'responsibility for something wrong' and as the idea of 'blame'.

ⓔ All questions on fault require a definition, but as this answer demonstrates, it does not have to be lengthy or detailed.

It could be argued that fault is fundamentally important in criminal law because of the terminology used; words such as 'guilt' and 'punishment' clearly suggest the idea of fault or wrongdoing. Punishments vary depending for the most part on how serious the crime is (e.g. life for murder, 6 months for battery).

Fault is also present in *mens rea*. It is fundamental to criminal law that a person cannot be held responsible for a crime unless he or she has the necessary mental awareness — a 'guilty mind'. The criminal law recognises different levels of *mens rea*. Intent is where you make something your aim and purpose (e.g. *Mohan*). But the criminal law also recognises that the person who acts with oblique intent is just as much at fault. It was confirmed in the cases of *Nedrick* and *Woollin* that people who knew that death or serious injury was virtually certain to result from their actions and yet continued can be regarded as having intended that consequence.

Recklessness involves knowing that there is a risk and yet continuing with the action (*Cunningham*). The person who does this is still at fault and recklessness is part of the *mens rea* for many crimes (e.g. assault and criminal damage). It was confirmed in *R* v *G* that recklessness always has to be subjective.

The rules on *actus reus* also demonstrate that fault is a fundamental principle, for example in the requirement that the action must be a voluntary one (e.g. *Hill* v *Baxter*). An omission will not usually form the *actus reus*, but the law recognises that in some situations a person who fails to act is at fault. For example, in *Stone and Dobinson* the defendants were at fault because they had had assumed responsibility for someone and in *Pitwood* the defendant had a contractual duty to close the gate.

Defences also illustrate that fault is fundamental. For example, a person who kills deliberately as a result of an abnormality of mental functioning could be considered less at fault and therefore guilty of manslaughter rather than murder (e.g. *Byrne*). Likewise the person who kills deliberately as a result of having a justifiable sense of being seriously wronged or because of fear of serious violence and who pleads loss of control under s.54 of the Coroners and Justice Act 2009 could also be considered to be less at fault and so guilty of manslaughter. A person who acts in self-defence and uses reasonable force as in *Bird* or *Palmer* is considered not to be at fault at all and has a complete defence.

ⓔ The answer identifies a number of aspects of criminal law which illustrate the importance of fault. Notice how in each paragraph the answer makes the link to fault and directly answers the question.

It could also be argued that fault is of fundamental importance in tort law. A person will only be liable in negligence if his or her behaviour falls below the standard of the reasonable man as confirmed in *Blythe* v *Birmingham*. The person who knows that the consequences of an accident would be very serious would clearly be at fault if he or she did not try to prevent it (e.g. *Paris* v *Stepney*). A similar fault element operates in the Occupiers' Liability Acts. An occupier who fails to take reasonable care to make sure that a lawful visitor is reasonably safe (OLA 1957 s.2(2)) is clearly at fault. An occupier is considered to be less at fault if a trespasser is injured than if the victim is a lawful visitor. This is reflected in the Occupiers' Liability Act 1984, which limits the duty owed to trespassers by occupiers.

ⓔ There is no need for the answer to deal with both crime and tort, but a brief paragraph like this one is valuable because it adds to the range of the answer.

However, there is some evidence to suggest that fault is not consistently followed and may not always be so fundamental. For example, in criminal law there are particular issues with involuntary manslaughter, which despite being a serious offence does not seem to fit in with the rules on *mens rea*. For unlawful and dangerous act manslaughter it is only necessary to prove the *mens rea* for the unlawful act, which in a case like *Mitchell* might only be that of battery. Also, although the act has to be dangerous, it is clear from *Church* that this is judged by the objective standard of what the sober and reasonable person would regard as dangerous. In gross negligence manslaughter the basis of liability is extreme negligence and it is clear from the judgement in *Prentice* that this can be determined objectively. The definition in *Bateman*, approved in *Adomako*, that it is such disregard for the life and safety of others as to amount to a crime does not clearly identify the actual mental element required to determine guilt.

ⓔ The answer moves onto the second part of the question — the arguments that fault is not always important.

The existence of strict and absolute liability offences most clearly demonstrate that fault is not always required in criminal law. In cases like *Callow* v *Tillstone* and *Harrow* v *Shah* it does not seem fair that the defendants should be guilty when they tried hard to avoid the commission of the offence. Absolute liability offences as illustrated by *Larsonneur* and *Winzar* seem to have even less of a fault element because in both cases the defendants were being controlled by other people and they could not prevent being placed in the circumstances which constituted the offence.

The justification for such offences is that they are of a minor, mainly regulatory nature and that they help to protect the public. This argument was advanced by the social scientist Barbara Wootten and also used by the House of Lords in *Wings* v *Ellis*. There is the additional argument that strict liability saves time and expense. In *Gammon* v *Att. Gen. of Hong Kong* it was argued that if *mens rea* had to be proved in every regulatory offence, the administration of justice might come to a complete standstill. A further argument is that it is much easier to prove corporate liability in strict liability offences.

Against this is the argument that even minor offences carry a stigma and for a business the consequence of conviction is likely to be loss of trade. Morally it seems wrong to convict people without having to prove that they are at fault.

(e) The question does not, as some do, specifically ask for a discussion of the merits or otherwise of liability based on fault, but it is appropriate in a question that asks for a discussion that a brief mention is made of the justifications for strict liability and the arguments against.

A further issue is that criminal law does not make a distinction between intention and motive. A person who kills out of compassion, as in the case of *Cox,* would seem to be less at fault than the person who kills out of hatred and yet the law treats them both in the same way as being guilty of murder if they intend to kill or cause serious harm.

Mandatory sentences for murder under the Criminal Justice Act 2003 also seem to go against the fault principle because they do not allow judges to take into account the particular circumstances of the defendant.

There is also evidence that fault is not fundamental in tort. The idea of vicarious liability goes completely against the fault principle and it seems unfair that an employer who forbids his or her employee from doing something will actually be responsible for that tort as in *Limpus* v *London General Buses* or *Rose* v *Plenty*. Also the basis of liability in nuisance is not really fault, but the need to strike a balance between two legitimate uses of land. A fault element only really appears through malice (e.g. *Christie* v *Davey*). The tort in *Rylands* v *Fletcher* is one of strict liability and there is no need to prove fault at all, though it should be pointed out that judges have consistently restricted the circumstances in which the tort can be used and it is now limited by *Transco* v *Stockport* to uses of land which are 'extraordinary and unusual'.

In conclusion, although fault does seem fundamental in most aspects of criminal law and also in aspects of tort, there are exceptions.

(e) **29 or 30/30 marks awarded.** This is a wide-ranging answer which uses many examples from a variety of areas of law. It is predominantly based on crime, but it also refers to examples from tort.

The answer is well balanced, covering arguments for and against the suggestion that fault is a fundamental principle. It also offers some evaluative comment on whether or not fault should be important, though this is kept brief as it is not a specific requirement of the question.

The conclusion is rather brief and abrupt, as if the student has run out of time, but the arguments in the body of the answer are clear and as a whole the answer is well structured.

Question 5 **Balancing conflicting interests**

To what extent does English law achieve a balancing of conflicting interests? (30 marks)

(e) This question asks 'to what extent'. This phrase requires you to consider evidence and make a judgement. The whole question needs to be a discussion of whether or not conflicting interests are appropriately balanced. This cannot be done without reference to specific issues and probably the best approach is to give a series of examples, which could be taken from any part of the specification or from issues currently in the news.

A-grade answer

In any society there are conflicting interests and one role of the law is to ensure that all interests are considered and balanced in both its creation and its enforcement.

A balancing of competing interests is achieved to some extent by the process of making an Act of Parliament. The Green Paper stage encourages consultation with interested parties and the bill stages require debates in both Houses of Parliament during which many interests will be considered. However, it can be argued that at each of these stages not all interests will be truly balanced because the more powerful interest groups (e.g. businesses or trade unions) may influence the process more than they should.

Parliament may also enact protective legislation to redress an unequal balance. Examples include the Consumer Protection Act 1987 which imposes strict liability on a producer in respect of damage caused by dangerous products and the Sales and Supply of Goods Act 1994 which implies conditions into consumer contracts. However, it is arguable whether a true balance of competing interests is achieved by such legislation because, as Phil Harris points out, the rights are dependable on individual enforcement, which requires consumers to have the legal knowledge and financial means to bring an action.

Government departments are also required to balance competing interests when exercising their powers. In 2012 the Department for the Environment, Food and Rural Affairs changed a decision, exercised under the Wildlife Act, to reduce the numbers of buzzards in order to protect pheasants being bred for shooting. Conservation groups and the public questioned the decision on the basis that the wildlife minister, a keen member of the shooting community, had favoured the interests of the pheasant shoots.

The law also provides courts and tribunals where conflicts of interest can be resolved. For a balance of interests to take place in the courts there must be access to the courts for all. However, access is often prevented by cost, as highlighted by Lord Woolf, and government funding for those unable to afford legal action has been cut consistently by successive governments since its introduction in 1949. The Legal Aid (Sentencing and Punishment of Offenders) Act 2012 seeks to reduce government funding by £350 million.

(e) This answer begins by considering the role of Parliament. It then looks at other state institutions, government departments and the courts. Notice that the approach adopted is to consider examples and to explore how far the examples illustrate that balance is being achieved.

In the nineteenth century, von Jhering suggested that society needed law to regulate the conflicts that would inevitably arise between the many different interests and argued that law acted as a mediator between these various competing interests. He was a utilitarian and could therefore be said to favour the public interest over the private. The US academic Roscoe Pound believed there are two types of interests — individual interests and social interests, and that a true balancing of interests can only happen when private interests are balanced against private interests and social interests are balanced against social interests.

The courts do not follow Roscoe Pound's theory, preferring to balance public interests against private interests. For example, in *Miller* v *Jackson*, Lord Denning approached the problem in terms of 'a conflict between the interests of the public at large and the interests of a private individual'. Denning concluded that the public interest in playing cricket outweighed the individual interest in not having balls hit into one's garden and refused to grant the injunction, although he did attempt to balance this by awarding damages. This issue could have been approached in terms of one individual's private interest in enjoying his garden against the private interest of a person in playing cricket.

e This answer considers theories in the middle rather than at the beginning, but the important point to note is that the theories are not simply described. Instead the answer comments critically on whether they contribute anything useful to the question that the answer has to address. The conclusion is that they do not really reflect the way in which the courts approach the issue, but by considering them the quality of the answer is enhanced significantly.

Another area involving conflict between public and private interests is the protection of human rights. The Human Rights Act 1998 seems to emphasise the private over the public interest. However, many of the rights have derogation clauses which allow the public interest to prevail. For example, Article 8 can be overridden in the interests of national security, public safety, the economic wellbeing of the country or the protection of health or morals. However, some rights in the European Convention are not derogable, for example Article 3, which protects the right not to be subjected to torture or to inhuman or degrading treatment or punishment.

Similarly, it can be argued that the courts have no preference for the public or private interests. In *A and others* v *Secretary of State for the Home Department* (2004), the House of Lords decided that the use of s.21 of the Anti-Terrorism, Crime and Security Act 2001 to detain foreign nationals without charge was unlawful despite the public interest arguments. Similarly, in *Marper* (2008) the European Court of Human Rights held that indefinite retention of DNA samples of innocent people breached Article 8 despite the public interest in protection from crime. However, the public interest in national security did prevail in 2012 when Abu Qatada, a radical Islamic preacher, was denied bail pending deportation proceedings.

Privacy cases usually require the courts to balance the public interest in freedom of expression with the individual interest in privacy. Again it can be argued the courts have no preference. The private interest prevailed in 2011 when the footballer Ryan Giggs was granted an injunction preventing publication of details of his extra-marital affairs. However, the public interest prevailed in *Rio Ferdinand* v *Mirror Group Newspapers* (2011) when the court refused to award damages in respect of a published article detailing his extra-marital affair. The Joint Committee on Privacy and Injunctions concluded in 2012 that the courts are getting the balance between the public and private interests right.

ⓔ The paragraph on privacy illustrates the requirement to assess the effectiveness of the balancing need. Judgements are made about effectiveness in the context of the private vs public debate.

The need for balance can also be seen in the law relating to criminal procedure. The public interest in the need to ensure public order and protect the lives and property of citizens must be balanced against the private interests of individual defendants to have a fair trial and the private needs of victims for justice. But frequent changes to the rules by successive governments suggest that the balance in this area is far from effective. For example, the Legal Aid (Sentencing and Punishment of Offenders) Act 2012 abolishes Indeterminate Sentences for Public Protection. These were introduced by the Criminal Justice Act 2003 which provided for the detention of offenders who had served their sentences but who in the court's opinion posed a significant risk to the public of serious harm by the commission of further specified offences.

Terrorism laws undergo continuous change in the attempt to balance competing interests. Following the terrorist attacks on 11 September 2001 emergency laws were passed allowing for indefinite detention without charge of foreign nationals suspected of terrorism. In 2004 the House of Lords held that these laws breached the suspects' human rights. The government responded by introducing control orders. Controversy concerning the severe restrictions imposed on an individual's liberty by control orders has resulted in their abolition and replacement in January 2012 with Terrorism Prevention and Investigation Measures. These are similar to control orders but less severe in that they cannot last for more than 2 years and suspects cannot be relocated to other areas. This change and the reduction in the maximum period someone can be held without charge from 28 days to 14 under the Protection of Freedoms Act 2012 appear to have shifted the balance in favour of individual rights and against the government. However, the courts are mindful of the need to assess risk on a case-by-case basis and in May 2012 Abu Qatada was refused bail pending his deportation appeal because of the high risk of him absconding and the resources that would then have to be employed to finding him, potentially during the Olympics.

In conclusion, it is evident that achieving balance is not easy but it is encouraging that even in areas where it is particularly difficult such as crime and terrorism the legislature and the courts are willing to change and adapt the rules in order to try to achieve the appropriate balance.

ⓔ **29 or 30/30 marks awarded.** This is a full and very well-evidenced answer. It displays understanding both of theoretical ideas and of the context provided by the institutions and law-making machinery and it explores a variety of relevant and topical examples. It also makes appropriate judgements on the effectiveness of the balance achieved. It would be assessed as sound.

Knowledge check answers

1 **(a)** The state.
  (b) Friends, family, religious bodies.
2 They both impose standards of conduct and they both use normative language.
3 A society in which many different views on moral issues are held.
4 They believed that the law should not interfere with acts done in private.
5 They believed that without legal enforcement of moral standards society would disintegrate.
6 It recognises that people should be able to do what they want in private.
7 *Shaw* v *DPP* (1962) and *R* v *Gibson* (1990).
8 Because assisted suicide is still a criminal offence punishable by imprisonment.
9 Jeremy Bentham.
10 Derogation clauses.
11 It goes against the rule of law to punish people without establishing through the courts that they have broken the law.
12 In both cases there was a perception of judicial bias. According to natural justice no one should be a judge in his/her own cause.
13 Corrective justice.
14 *R* v *Twomey* (2010).
15 Substantive justice and distributive justice.
16 The power to depart from its previous decisions when it appears 'right to do so'.
17 All courts.

18 The Court of Appeal hears more cases.
19 The purposive approach.
20 It requires judges to interpret domestic legislation so that it is compatible with the European Convention on Human Rights.
21 Formulation of policy is political and the role of the elected Parliament.
22 The literal rule.
23 Because it applies to events which have already taken place.
24 Voluntary act, automatism and duress, causation and omissions.
25 Because the defendant is considered to be less at fault.
26 The fault element does not equate with the consequence.
27 There is no fault requirement in terms of *mens rea*.
28 They require an automatic sentence rather than allowing the judge to consider the actual degree of fault by the defendant.
29 Because they had done all that the reasonable man would have done.
30 The defendants had not done what the reasonable man would have done.
31 Because the victim has not voluntarily accepted the risk.
32 Defendants are only liable for damage of a foreseeable type.
33 He honestly and reasonably believed the victim to be aged 15.
34 The public interest was in being able to play cricket. The private interest was in not having balls hit into one's garden.
35 To balance interests by protecting a weaker party.
36 Freedom of expression.
37 The courts cannot balance conflicting interests if people cannot afford to use them.
38 The interests of society, of the defendant and of the victim.
39 Public safety.
40 The availability of affordable insurance.